Y0-CAX-954

Kenneth Grahame's

THE WIND IN THE WILLOWS

Teacher Guide

Maggi Windhorst & Cheryl Lowe

MEMORIA PRESS

MEMORIA PRESS
www.MemoriaPress.com

Kenneth Grahame's
THE WIND IN THE WILLOWS
TEACHER GUIDE
Maggi Windhorst & Cheryl Lowe

ISBN 978-1-5477-0215-2

Second Edition © 2019 Memoria Press

Cover Illustration: Starr Steinbach

All rights reserved. No part of this book may be reproduced in any form
by any means without written permission from the publisher.

CONTENTS

How to Use This Study Guide With the Text

A Step-By-Step Plan

INTRODUCTION AND PREPARATION

A. First read through the Notes & Instructions to Teacher (or Student).

B. Read the two introductory essays, "Taking With Us What Matters" and "Four Stages to the Central One Idea."

C. Read "How to Mark a Book."

D. Read and study the Introduction.

E. Read and study the Basic Features & Background.

BEGIN TEXT PROPER

1. Begin with the Pre-Grammar section. This prepares the mind, at least in some small way, for the reading and study of *The Wind in the Willows*, and, ideally, for the Central One Idea.

2. Read through the Reading Notes closely, stopping occasionally to discuss or clarify.

3. Next, try to define as many words from the Words to Be Defined section as possible. You may not be able to answer all of them before reading the text, but this will improve your understanding and comprehension of the text when you begin reading.

4. Now, read thoroughly and well the particular section of *The Wind in the Willows* delineated by the Study Guide (i.e., Chapter 3), marking the text in key places according to the method taught in "How to Mark a Book."

5. Return to the Study Guide and finish defining any remaining Words to Be Defined. If need be, refer to the word in the text for contextual help, or in a dictionary, of course.

6. Answer the Comprehension Questions, stopping to discuss and referring back to the text when necessary.

7. Answer the Socratic Discussion Questions, taking additional time to discuss and contemplate, referring back to the text often or when necessary.

8. Complete the Rhetoric | Expression — Central One Idea section. Take the time to consider and reflect upon the Central One Idea; discuss freely, making room for disagreement as well as convergence.

9. Complete the Essay Option at your teacher's discretion.

10. Repeat steps 1-9 for each section.

Notes & Instructions to Teacher

- Though I recommend that, ideally, your students complete the entire Study Guide in conjunction with reading and discussing the text, the Study Guide is also meant to be **adapted to your particular context**. This means you should feel comfortable using the Study Guide to best suit the needs of you and your student(s)—in a manner that fits your family or class size, schedule, number of meetings per week, time for grading, time allowed for discussion, and total time for the unit, etc. This may mean that you will choose to assign fewer vocabulary words and questions, etc. This is fine, and I encourage it. I have written the guides comprehensively to provide a maximum number of notes, words, and questions—so that you will be able to assign fewer if need be, rather than wishing there were more.

- The Introduction gives a biography of the author, Kenneth Grahame.

- You will notice that many questions ask the student to quote a line(s) from the text in his answer. This will help develop the student's ability to find evidence in the text to support his answer. It will also develop the practice and art of synthesizing quoted material into his written argument, which is an important skill for essay writing.

- The Reading Notes section contains some helpful notes and facts along with some challenging vocabulary words. Some of the vocabulary words appear in the Reading Notes in order to keep the number of words in the Words to Be Defined section manageable.

- The Words to Be Defined section contains higher-level words selected because they are both *challenging* and *useful* for the student to learn and memorize.

- Please note that the number of blank lines printed per question for the Comprehension and Socratic Discussion Questions are *loosely approximate*. The student should answer the question thoroughly and accurately without worrying whether he fills all the lines. Accuracy and clarity are much more important than just "filling the space." If lines are left blank, that is fine! Or if a student needs to write beyond the lines, that is also fine!

- Some of the essay prompts tend toward a shorter essay, and some toward a longer. Both short essays (1 page) and long essays (2-4 pages) are useful and helpful, depending on the intent and purpose. Four lined pages are included to provide a maximum range of space.

- As a kind of "final achievement" that celebrates the reading of the novel and completion of the Study Guide, please have your student(s) complete the Memorization & Recitation section at the end of the Study Guide. Additionally, this section will allow the student to move on from the novel with a special part of *The Wind in the Willows* in his heart.

Taking With Us What Matters

The Transformative Power of Reading for the Central One Idea

David M. Wright

Sometimes our study of literature resembles a kind of clinical laboratory lesson. We encircle the text in our white coats ready to dissect the story (or poem) like a dead animal. Or if this sounds too invasive or scientific, then we *analyze* the text in order to extract the "elements of literature" (the title of a recent bigpress high school English textbook)—to know the work by studying its parts. Or perhaps we analyze simply to have a meaningful artistic engagement with the text.

All of these, though, fall short of what our true purpose and intent should be when reading a Great Work. But ironically, this very purpose may be the most overlooked. This brings to mind a few similar yet related aphorisms: What we go about searching everywhere for is often right in front of us or within us; overstimulate the senses, and they sense less; keep it simple; less is more.

What we are missing in our modern study of literature is a conscious effort to uncover the soul of the work, the *essence* from which it derives its being—a fundamental, ontological reality that I have named the *Central One Idea*. Searching for and determining the Central One Idea profoundly shapes our interaction with the work and the trajectory of our study. There are seven reasons why this is so.

First, by doing so, we honor the work. Just as we notice an innate hierarchy in the natural world, in societies, organizations, and families, we insist that a kind of hierarchy exists in the work as well: there is one idea at the heart of the story; one idea burning as the sun in its solar system, with many planets (literary elements) in rotation around it. This idea gives the work its ultimate meaning and its greatest expression. In this idea, the other elements find their raison d'être.

Second, I often ask my students, "What's in a title?" to which they reply, "Everything." Then I ask, "What's in a name?" and they promptly reply, "Everything." I repeatedly ask this not only because repetition is the mother of learning, but because I do not want them to miss what is right in front of them: The title of a work often hints at, points toward, or outright expresses the Central One Idea.

Why parents think deeply about the name they give their child reiterates this point. Names matter; they represent the potential character and nature of the child. In this spirit, I chose the name Central One Idea carefully so that its nature and purpose would be inherent. It does not roll too quickly off the tongue, but instead demands a certain level of consciousness to express. It is *central*; it is *one*; and it is an *idea*. In other words, it is central to the work and stands above other ideas, determined then to be subideas; it is singular; and it is a complete idea, that is, a proposition with a subject and a predicate, not just a subject.

Third, when we consider the essay, the academic paper, the dissertation, or any other nonfiction work, we insist that it must have a *thesis*. The thesis is everything to that particular work—so much so that, ontologically, the work derives its being from its thesis. It is no mystery why many high school and college English teachers demand that their students underline the thesis in their papers—to combat their students' shoddy understanding of what a thesis is and why it is so important.

In the nonfiction genre especially, the title almost always encapsulates the thesis. Take, for example, the academic bestseller some years ago: *Guns, Germs, and Steel: The Fates of Human Societies.* Here Jared Diamond argues that the varied developments of human societies on different continents are the result of environmental determinism—geography, population, and agriculture—and more specifically, that Eurasian technological and economic rise and dominance stemmed from their superior weapons (guns), their diseases which weakened indigenous populations (germs), and their centralized government which fostered powerful military organizations (steel). One can almost read the title, absorb the thesis, and devote 500 pages to something else, say Hugo's *Les Misérables*.

Is a novel, play, or poem really any different than a work of nonfiction? Does not fiction express a thesis just as nonfiction? I believe it does. If not explicitly, then implicitly—for it must express *something*, and that *something* is the Central One Idea. As well, that essential idea is that which *compels* the author to put pen to paper, or the artist to put brush to canvas. The novel, poem, or painting is simply (and profoundly) the artistic medium or rendering of the idea.

So what, then, does a Central One Idea look like? In Charles Dickens' *Hard Times*, the owner of a school instructs his students in "nothing but facts" and finally realizes that his program ruins the humanity of his students. The Central One Idea: Life should be lived with imagination rather than by an overemphasis on logic and cold facts. In Herman Melville's *Billy Budd*, a young sailor is falsely accused of mutiny. The Central One Idea: Human nature is both pure and corrupt, just as physical nature is both beautiful and harsh. (Yes, these could be said in various ways; and yes, others could be argued for, but I'll get to this in point six.)

Fourth, reading for the Central One Idea moves our methodology back toward the classical and medieval, toward what C. S. Lewis called "the discarded image." In previous ages, the *idea* and *truth* had a kind of unity and primacy that is lost in modernity. I think here of Plato and his forms, Aristotle and his organized classification of reality, Dante and his fixed and ordered cosmology. The moderns prefer fragmentation, subjectivism, and deconstruction of both the idea and truth. More comfortable with truth shattered into shards, this age insists that reality is broken and disconnected, not whole and unified.

Approaching a work of literature with this broken and distant framework means students are uncomfortable asserting any one truth about a story—too afraid to insist: *This is the fundamental idea that drives this novel*. They are more satisfied pointing out elements in the work that stand out to them rather than ascribing primacy to any one; or more often, they prefer expressing *how the novel makes them feel*. As well, they might focus undue attention on a character that they like or dislike based on whether the character behaves in a way acceptable to contemporary (politically correct) standards.

Fifth, the Central One Idea might be the primary factor in the movement from novel to *Great Book*. It is difficult to find any Great Book without a prominent Central One Idea. The book becomes timeless and great for two reasons—one, it has an important Central One Idea; and two, because that idea is expressed with masterful artistry, form, and beauty.

Sixth, determining the Central One Idea engenders logical thought and rhetorical speech. It demands close reading and analysis, supporting evidence and proof; it generates critical discussion and rhetorical writing. The nous (in patristic thought, the eye of the heart) of a work is not always easy to find. Sometimes it is everywhere present but cannot be directly seen. Sometimes it has to be wrestled for in the midst of competing ideas. Sometimes it seems too obvious and simple. But nonetheless, teaching the work in this method requires the student to stake a claim for one central idea. The student must then defend his or her Central One Idea with evidence from the text, the Study Guide, scholarly sources, or his/her own logic. And this stimulates fruitful class discussion and debate, and leads directly to the essay and composition.

Finally, reading for the Central One Idea is the essential way to study literature because it is an act of discovery. Since we desire by nature to know, we experience joy when we discover new things and complete gaps in logical sequences. We seek so that we may find. The joy of learning comes from the Elysian fount of discovery. May we let our search for and insistence upon the Central One Idea become the logos of our study of the Great Works, and find there wisdom and virtue.

Four Stages to the Central One Idea

Using the Trivium to Uncover the Heart of a Work

David M. Wright

UNDERSTANDING THE SEQUENCE AND STAGES OF THE STUDY GUIDE

Because discovering and internalizing the Central One Idea in a Great Work is vital for a proper reading and for cultivating wisdom and virtue, it necessitates that the Study Guide embody this conceptual framework. Thus, the guide is written in such a way as to lead the student (and teacher) through four stages to the acquisition and expression of the Central One Idea.

The four-stage sequence is rooted in the trivium—grammar, logic, and rhetoric—which has vestiges from the order and way of learning spanning several ages since antiquity. In the trivium, grammar is language; logic (dialectic) is thought; and rhetoric is expression. Put another way, in the grammar stage, one accumulates the fundamental elements, features, and facts of a body of knowledge. In the logic stage, one arranges, connects, organizes, compares, and reasons with the facts learned and draws a conclusion(s). In the rhetoric stage, one expresses that conclusion/truth to others.

Sister Miriam Joseph defined the trivium as the three arts of language pertaining to the mind: grammar is the art of inventing and combining symbols; logic is the art of thinking; and rhetoric is the art of communication.[1] She also states it in this way: grammar is concerned with the thing-as-it-is-symbolized; logic is concerned with the thing-as-it-is-known; and rhetoric is concerned with the thing-as-it-is-communicated.[2]

The trivium, she says, is the organon, or instrument, of all education at all levels because the arts of grammar, logic, and rhetoric govern the means of communication—namely reading, writing, speaking, and listening. She adds, "Because communication involves the simultaneous exercise of logic, grammar, and rhetoric, these three arts are the

fundamental arts of education, of teaching, and of being taught. Accordingly, they must be practiced simultaneously by the teacher and pupil."[3]

As well, the trivium is a movement from distinct parts into synthesized whole. The three stages guide the student to relate the facts learned into a unified, organic whole. This encompasses the aim and purpose of this guide—to move from elements and parts toward the unity and wholeness of the Central One Idea.

Marguerite McGlinn, introducing Joseph's work, says, "The trivium teaches us that language evolves from the very nature of being human. … We invent symbols to express the range of practical, theoretical, and poetical experiences that make up our existence. … Words are characterized by their relationship to being and to each other. When a speaker or writer uses a word, thus assigning it a particular meaning, it becomes a term and enters the realm of logic. … The linguistic symbol is then translated into a logical entity ready to take its place in a proposition."[4]

We can see, then, that the trivium has much to do with being human, with negotiating our lives. It has an ontological reality within us through our use of reason and language. The four-stage sequence developed for these Study Guides is trivium-based because the trivium embodies how we think, how we learn, and how we communicate.

In our particular context of studying a Great Work, the teacher has firmly in mind the abstract singular truth that he or she wishes the student to learn, which is the Central One Idea of the work. Several other salient ideas inherent in the work will be discovered and learned along the way, but it is the Central One Idea that is the ultimate aim and purpose of the study. Knowing the destination is vitally important in this four-stage sequence. Though popular culture may be fond of saying, "It's not the destination that counts, but the journey"— nothing should be further from classical teaching

---

[1] Sister Miriam Joseph. *The Trivium: The Liberal Arts of Logic, Grammar, and Rhetoric.* Ed. by Marguerite McGlinn. (Philadelphia: Paul Dry Books, 2002) 3.
[2] Ibid., 9.

[3] Ibid., 6-7.
[4] Ibid., viii.

and learning. Both the journey and the destination count, but especially the destination, which is the understanding and expression of the idea.

THE FOUR STAGES PROCEED AS FOLLOWS:

Stage 1: Pre-Grammar | Preparation

To begin, the Pre-Grammar stage prepares the student for receiving and understanding the Central One Idea by invoking his prior knowledge, experience, or interests concerning that idea. Just as Socrates believed that the truth he wanted his interlocutor to understand was already within him, in some way or part, the Central One Idea is already the soil within the student. Thus, it is helpful to cultivate the soil in preparation for planting the seed. In this preparatory stage, the student is merely asked a few questions about something related to the Central One Idea, or simply about the basic plot or subject of the work—to set him thinking in a certain direction. The Study Guide features two or three questions that aim to do this, but may be supplemented with different questions or with discussion as the teacher sees fit. This is the shortest stage and can take as little as five minutes (though fine if longer).

Stage 2: Grammar | Presentation

In the Grammar stage, the student is presented with and discovers essential facts, elements, and features of the story (or play, poem, etc.). Here the student encounters many useful facts in the Reading Notes and learns new vocabulary words in the Words to Be Defined section. In addition, the student becomes grounded in the basic features of the story through the Comprehension Questions and learns new literary and rhetorical terms (that appear in bold throughout both the Grammar and Logic sections). In this stage, the student is presented with the basic grammatical units—facts, elements, features, ideas—that comprise the work. She begins to familiarize her mind with new subject matter. New *types* or *particulars* are presented and discovered here.

Stage 3: Logic | Dialectic

In the Logic stage, the student *reasons* with the facts, elements, and features of the story/poem; sorts arranges, compares, and connects ideas— and begins to uncover and determine the Central One Idea. He *compares* the new ideas and facts with similar things already in the mind, which gives rise to new conclusions. Importantly, the final conclusion, the Central One Idea, is often an *abstract* or *general* truth, though it may be expressed by means of a story's particulars, such as a character's action and discovery, etc. The best method for leading the student toward this new abstract truth is through the Socratic method. Hence, this stage features Socratic Discussion Questions, which are different than the Comprehension Questions in the previous stage because they go further up and further in to abstract thought. Simply put, they are deeper questions with the intent of leading the student toward the Central One Idea.

At the end of this stage, the student should be ready to make a determination of what he thinks is the Central One Idea. This is not always easy, but the student should be encouraged to take this step, a kind of "leap of faith"—though not a huge leap over a dark chasm, but a short step relying on logic and evidence from close reading, work in the Study Guide, and attentive perception and reflection.

It should be noted here that this general truth may now be exemplified in new cases and applied to new circumstances, one of which will be the expression and defense of the Central One Idea in the rhetoric stage.

Stage 4: Rhetoric | Expression

In the final stage, the student expresses what she believes to be the Central One Idea. The student's ability to organize and express her thoughts is an important skill in the Rhetoric/Expression stage.

In this section, the first question asks the student to briefly summarize the plot, and the second question asks the student to express the Central One Idea in a complete sentence. The reason for this is so the student will be forced to distinguish between a plot summary and the Central One Idea. The two are quite different. The former, of course, concerns the sequence of events in the story. The latter concerns a larger *abstract* truth—the central proposition at the heart of the story.

The third question asks the student to list three supporting points for her determination of the Central One Idea. Finally, there is space in the workbook for the student to write the teacher's version of the Central One Idea—which is helpful for several reasons, the first of which is that it enables the student to draw a comparison.

In the last section of the Rhetoric stage, the student is presented with the opportunity to write an essay—to express her Central One Idea—the thesis she must argue for and defend in her essay. This improves the student's writing skills and increases her rhetorical abilities.

How to Mark a Book

1. Underline all important passages.

2. Place a vertical line in the margin next to very important passages which you have already underlined.

3. Place an asterisk next to key passages which you have already underlined and which already have a vertical line in the margin next to them.

4. Make notes in the margin to indicate important points made in the text.

Example:

Mortimer Adler points out in *How to Read a Book* that reading is a conversation between the reader and the author. You read a book, presumably, in order to learn from the author, but this process is not just a passive process on your part. The reader understands, questions, and sometimes must argue with the author. The highest respect you can pay an author is to respond—positively or negatively—to him. The markings in a book are an expression of that.

Reading is a conversation

There are several devices that can be used in marking a book or article. Each has a different purpose. First, you should underline important or forceful parts of the reading. This will normally be done on about 15 percent of the text. However, no more than 30 or 40 percent of text, even in a very key reading, should be underlined.

Underline

Second, you should use vertical lines in the outside margin to emphasize text that you have already underlined. Normally, no more than about 10 to 25 percent of the text you underlined in any reading should be marked in this way.

Use vertical lines

Third, you should mark any text that stands out as one of the one to three most important statements in the book, chapter, or article. This will be text you have already marked with a vertical line in the margin. Mark it again, using a star, asterisk, or other doodad. If the passage is truly extraordinary, you can mark it with two of these markings. If it is life-changing, you might even try three, but you should find one of these very seldom.

Use asterisks

*

Fourth, you should make notes and write numbers in the margin. Making notes can reduce a complicated part of the text to a simple statement or record a question that a passage raises in your mind. Numbers can also be used to record a sequence of major points or to indicate where else in the book the author makes the same points.

Write notes (or numbers) in the margin.

You can also put a double line for any text that is not only important, but quotable or aptly stated.

‖

INTRODUCTION

KENNETH GRAHAME (MARCH 8, 1859-JULY 6, 1932)

Born in Edinburgh, Scotland, on March 8, 1859, Kenneth Grahame is the celebrated author of *The Wind in the Willows*. He was the third child of Bessie and Cunningham Grahame. Soon after his birth, his father received a new position and moved the family to Argyll. When Grahame was five, his mother died of scarlet fever just after giving birth to his brother. As a result, his father turned to alcohol and was unable to care for the four children. Grahame and his siblings moved to the home of their grandmother, Mary Inglis, in England. They lived in a grand country home with gardens and orchards. He attended church and boated on the nearby River Thames. He spent time in the surrounding fields and woods, which would influence his creativity.

Grahame's father attempted to recover and moved the children back home. However, after a relapse, the children returned to living with their grandmother, while their father departed for France. The children did not have contact with their father again.

Grahame went to boarding school and attended St. Edward's in Oxford. He was a successful student, earning awards in Latin, theology, and rugby. Grahame had a great desire to attend college, but he lacked the financial means to study at Oxford and instead took a job at the Bank of England in London.

Though Grahame was extremely successful and rising in his position at the bank, he began to write and submit articles and stories to various publications. His first story was published in 1888. His most famous short story, "The Reluctant Dragon," was published in 1898. Grahame's stories of children in *The Golden Age* and its sequel, *Dream Days*, brought him critical acclaim. He had earned himself a place in London's literary scene.

On July 22, 1899, Grahame married Elspeth Thomson. Their marriage was strained, and they often spent time apart. They had one son, Alistair, born in 1900. Known as "Mouse" by his parents, he was born sickly; he was blind in one eye and had a severe squint in the other. As he grew up, his behavior was problematic.

In 1903, while working at the bank, a man approached Grahame. After an odd exchange, the man pulled out a gun and shot at Grahame three times. Bank employees wrestled the man to the floor, and he was carried off in a straitjacket. Though all shots missed Grahame, the event had a profound effect on him, leaving him with the feeling that the outside world was not a safe place.

In an effort to connect with his son, Grahame began telling Alistair bedtime stories about the adventures of Mole, Badger, Toad, and Rat. Many scholars believe these stories were lessons meant to teach his son about the world, maturity, and respectability. Grahame called on the memories of his childhood in the country to create the setting of the stories. First attempts at publication were turned down. When *The Wind in the Willows* was finally published in 1908, it received terrible reviews. This changed, however, when Grahame sent a copy to U.S. President Theodore Roosevelt. The president loved it and sent it to an American publisher, where book sales flourished and made it a huge success.

Though his writing career was successful, Grahame's relationships at home continued to be difficult. Alistair's struggles at school contributed to a deteriorating emotional condition that led to his death shortly before his twentieth birthday in 1920. It is believed that Alistair committed suicide, though the death was ruled an accident. This had a deep impact on Grahame, and he wrote very little afterward. He died on July 6, 1932, and was buried beside his son's grave.

BASIC FEATURES & BACKGROUND

LITERARY TERMS

1. **alliteration** – the repetition of beginning sounds; e.g., "the diffident and delaying dog-rose stepped delicately on the stage"

2. **allusion** – a reference to any person, place, or thing (literary, historical, or actual)

3. **anthropomorphized** – giving animals humanlike qualities

4. **characters** – those taking part in the story

5. **epiphany** – a moment of insight, discovery, or revelation

6. **foreshadowing** – the use of indicative words or phrases that hint at something that will happen in the story; it sets the stage for the event without revealing the story or spoiling the suspense

7. **imagery** – a word or series of words referring to any sensory experience; direct or literal re-creation of physical experience

8. **metaphor** – a direct comparison between two unlike things (does not use *like, as,* or *than*); shows that something unknown can be understood because it is similar to something known

9. **onomatopoeia** – words created from the sound they make (e.g., bang, crack, hiss)

10. **personification** – giving humanlike qualities to objects or ideas

11. **plot** – a series of actions or related events that move the story forward

12. **setting** – the time and place of a literary work

13. **simile** – the comparison of two unlike things with the use of *like, as,* or *than*; shows that something unknown can be understood because it is similar to something known

CHARACTERS

1. **Mole** – A trusting, childlike underground dweller, moving up and out into the world above to experience life in the open air. He is naïve, knowing very little of the world, and must be taught. He is wide-eyed and ready to embrace new experiences and people.

2. **Ratty** – An experienced and knowledgeable water rat, living by the river. He has an abundance of wisdom to share. He understands the world and knows where he belongs in it. He befriends Mole and invites Mole to live with him.

3. **Badger** – An elderly animal, sober and reserved, that lives in the Wild Wood. He has moved beyond the influences and social dictates of the world and lives as he sees fit.

4. **Otter** – A social riverbank animal that enjoys sharing the local gossip. He is a father and a friend of Ratty.

5. **Toad** – A fast-moving, adventure-seeking animal, living in his ancestral home by the river. He is outgoing and friendly, though very self-centered.

SETTING

The Wind in the Willows does not have a specific setting. It creates a world where animals talk and interact with each other and possess human traits, living just beyond the human world. Though no specific location is given, it is likely the southeastern part of England with meadows, a river, farms, villages, and forests.

In the novel, Grahame creates distinctive realms. Underground places such as Mole's hole and Badger's home represent the inner self, a character's private thoughts that are shared with a trusted few. The river bank represents the home life, the safe places where everyone there is friendly and familiar. The Wild Wood is the larger community, where some of the people are known and interacted with, but not to be trusted. Dangers lurk in the Wild Wood, and one must be alert. The last realm is the Wide World, described by Rat to Mole as "something that doesn't matter, either to you or me. I've never been there, and I'm never going, nor you either, if you've got any sense at all. Don't ever refer to it again, please." The Wide World is unknown, unpredictable, and filled with humans.

PART ONE

Chapters 1-4

PRE-GRAMMAR | Preparation

Prepare the student for understanding the Central One Idea
by drawing upon his or her prior knowledge or experience.

1. Think of a fable where an animal was the main character. What were some of the traits the animal was given, and how did those traits shape the story?

    _____

    _____

    _____

    _____

    _____

    _____

    _____

2. What kind of animal would you pick to represent yourself? What qualities does that animal have that represent you?

    _____

    _____

    _____

    _____

    _____

    _____

    _____

3. Make a list of people who have influenced your life—those who have taught or coached you. Choose one and tell what lessons you have learned from this person.

    _____

    _____

    _____

    _____

    _____

    _____

GRAMMAR | Presentation
LOGIC | Dialectic

In the Grammar section, the student is presented with and discovers essential facts, elements, and features of the novel. In the Logic section, the student reasons with the facts, elements, and features of the novel; invents, sorts, arranges, compares, and connects ideas—and begins to uncover and determine the Central One Idea.

Chapter 1

READING NOTES

1. **Mole's hole** – Mole's secluded home underground

2. **hedgerows** – thick rows of bushes forming a hedge (a barrier or boundary)

3. **copses** – small groupings of trees

4. **bijou** – a beautiful jewel

5. **sculls** – a pair of oars used by a single rower

6. **River** – where the civilized animals such as Ratty, Otter, and Toad live; they call themselves "river-bankers"

7. **Wild Wood** – the world just past the River, where the animals can be friendly but are not to be trusted

8. **Wide World** – the outer world beyond the safety of the river bank; where the humans live

9. **weir** – a dam in a river, or a fence of broken branches or stakes put in a stream to catch fish

10. **punt** – to propel one's boat by using a pole against the river bottom

WORDS TO BE DEFINED

Definitions Bank

authoritatively	privacy
cellar; under	scorning; mocking
delicately; carefully	touched gently and affectionately
disdainful; disrespectful	unable to be filled or satisfied
liberated; freed	unplanned

---

1. Something up above was calling him **imperiously**

    authoritatively

2. soft breezes **caressed** his heated brow

    touched gently and affectionately

3. after the **seclusion** of the cellarage he had lived in

    privacy

4. after the seclusion of the **cellarage** he had lived in

    cellar; under

5. the impatient and **contemptuous** Mole

    disdainful; disrespectful

6. who trotted along the side of the hedge **chaffing** the other rabbits

    scorning; mocking

7. the **insatiable** sea

    unable to be filled or satisfied

8. the Mole stepped **gingerly** down

    delicately; carefully

9. This was an **impromptu** affair

    unplanned

10. the **emancipated** Mole

    liberated; freed

📖 *Read Chapter 1, marking the text in key places according to the method taught in "How to Mark a Book."*

COMPREHENSION QUESTIONS

1. Where has Mole lived his life to this point? What causes him to leave his home?

   To this point, Mole has lived in his underground hole by himself. The call of spring causes him

   to leave his home and dig up out of the earth into the sunshine of the meadow.

2. Mole first encounters rabbits when he gets above ground. What do they demand, and how does Mole respond?

   The first creatures Mole encounters are the rabbits that demand Mole pay sixpence for the

   privilege of passing by the road. Mole pushes through them, impatient and with contempt.

3. *He thought his happiness was complete when, as he meandered aimlessly along, suddenly he stood by the edge of a full-fed river. Never in his life had he seen a river before — this sleek, sinuous, full-bodied animal, chasing and chuckling, gripping things with a gurgle and leaving them with a laugh, to fling itself on fresh playmates that shook themselves free, and were caught and held again. All was a-shake and a-shiver — glints and gleams and sparkles, rustle and swirl, chatter and bubble.*

   In this passage, Grahame uses many literary elements to help the reader understand how "The Mole was bewitched, entranced, fascinated" upon seeing the river for the first time. Give an example of each element from the passage:

   a. Onomatopoeia: ___gurgle___

   b. Personification: ___chasing and chuckling, gripping things and leaving them with a laugh, fling on fresh playmates, caught and held, chatter___

   c. Alliteration: ___sleek, sinuous; chasing and chuckling; leaving them with a laugh; glints and gleams___

   d. Metaphor: ___The river is being compared to a full-bodied animal that is playful.___

4. How is the Water Rat described when Mole first sees him?

   Water Rat is described as having a brown little face with whiskers, a grave round face, and a

   twinkle in his eyes. He has small neat ears and thick silky hair.

5. Who says, "Believe me, my young friend, there is *nothing*—absolutely nothing—half so much worth doing as simply messing about in boats. Simply messing, messing—about—in—boats; messing—"? What does this say about the character?

   <u>Rat shows his love of boats and being on the water with this quote.</u>

6. What are the two animal etiquette rules mentioned in Chapter 1?

   <u>Rule 1: Never dwell on possible trouble ahead, or even allude to it. Rule 2: Never comment on</u>

   <u>the sudden disappearance of a friend.</u>

7. Though the reader does not meet Toad in Chapter 1, a lot is learned about his character in a conversation between Otter and the Rat. How do they describe Toad?

   <u>Toad is described as "such a good fellow," but with no stability. He takes up new adventures,</u>

   <u>but gets tired of them and moves on to something else.</u>

SOCRATIC DISCUSSION QUESTIONS (LOGIC | Dialectic)

1. Four worlds are described in Chapter 1. Explain what each world represents.

   a. Mole's hole: <u>Represents the inner self</u>

   b. river bank: <u>Represents the home and the place where people and things are</u>
      <u>familiar and trusted</u>

   c. Wild Wood: <u>Represents the community, the people and places a person interacts</u>
      <u>with, but does not know well</u>

   d. Wide World: <u>Represents the unknown world far from the safety and comfort of home</u>

2. Mole is inexperienced in life. What are some examples of his childlike behavior in Chapter 1?

He is spellbound by the river because he has never seen one. He does not pay attention to

details: He does not, at first, notice the Rat's boat, and he misses several items when packing

up the picnic basket. He steps into the boat without thinking of consequences because,

"Mole's whole heart went out to it at once, even though he did not yet fully understand its

uses." Mole gets absorbed in his surroundings and does not hear what the Rat is saying. Mole

asks the Rat about the different worlds. Mole causes the boat to flip in his childish grab for the

oars that he does not know how to use. Mole has to be escorted to bed.

3. From the moment that Mole steps into the Water Rat's boat, Ratty begins teaching Mole about the world. What are some of the lessons that Ratty teaches Mole?

Rat teaches about the three outer worlds and their boundaries. Rat explains the various

animals in the community. Through the oar incident, Ratty teaches Mole that he is

inexperienced and needs a mentor. "Not yet, my young friend," he said—"wait till you've had

a few lessons. It's not so easy as it looks."

4. After lunch, Mole impatiently and childishly reaches for the oars because he thinks he can manage them. What is the consequence of his action? Can you think of a time when you rushed to do something for which you were unprepared? What were the consequences?

When Mole jumps up and seizes the sculls so suddenly, the Rat is surprised and falls backwards

off his seat. Mole quickly takes Rat's place and, with false confidence, flings the sculls back and

misses the surface of the water, falling on Rat. Alarmed, Mole grabs the side of the boat and

tips the boat over.

5. At the end of the chapter, Grahame leaves the reader with a lesson on humility and giving grace through Mole and the Water Rat. How does Mole show humility? How does the Rat respond?

At the end of Chapter 1, Mole shows humility when he asks for Rat's forgiveness after tipping

the boat over. He says, "I am very sorry indeed for my foolish and ungrateful conduct. My

heart quite fails me when I think how I might have lost that beautiful luncheon-basket. Indeed,

I have been a complete ass, and I know it. Will you overlook it this once and forgive me, and

let things go on as before?"; Ratty forgives Mole and shows him grace. He says, "That's all

right, bless you!" Ratty invites Mole to come stay with him so that he can mentor Mole. He

says that he will teach Mole how to row and swim.

Chapter 2

READING NOTES

1. **Toad Hall** – Toad's ancestral home; the finest estate on the river

2. **the open road** – a long road one can follow with no destination in mind; Toad's idea of freedom and adventure

3. **common** – land owned or used by all the people of a community

4. **downs** – rolling, grassy land

5. **paddock** – a small enclosed field near a stable or house, used for exercising animals

WORDS TO BE DEFINED

Definitions Bank	
a space or pause between something reoccurring	granted
	outspoken; up-front
beyond remedy; hopeless	peaceful
friendly	
	talkative
frustrating; annoying	wasted
full of or expressing great joy	

1. he had a **candid** nature ___outspoken; up-front___

2. regret the wasted years that lie behind me, **squandered** in trivialities ___wasted___

3. your **amiable** friend ___friendly___

4. Naturally a **voluble** animal ___talkative___

5. Toad was by no means so **rapturous** about the simplicity of the primitive life _____
   ___full of or expressing great joy___

6. an **irredeemable** wreck ___beyond remedy; hopeless___

7. his face wore a **placid**, satisfied expression ___peaceful___

8. At **intervals** he was still heard to murmur ___a space or pause between something reoccurring___
   _____

9. that heavenly vision that has been **vouchsafed** me ___granted___

10. this **provoking** animal ___frustrating; annoying___

Read Chapter 2, marking the text in key places according to the method taught in "How to Mark a Book."

COMPREHENSION QUESTIONS

1. At the beginning of Chapter 2, what is consuming Rat's attention?

   At the start of the chapter, Rat's attention is on a little song he had composed about the

   ducks he had been observing.

   _____

   _____

2. Where does Mole ask Ratty to take him?

   Mole wants Rat to take him to meet Toad.

   _____

3. What additional information does Rat provide about Toad's character before taking him to Toad Hall?

Rat describes Toad by saying, "He is indeed the best of animals ... So simple, so good-natured, and so affectionate. Perhaps he's not very clever—we can't all be geniuses; and it may be that he is both boastful and conceited. But he has got some great qualities."

4. Toad tells Rat that he has given up boating for what latest adventure?

Toad has given up boating for "the open road" in a canary-yellow gypsy caravan.

5. How is Rat's reaction to the cart different from Mole's?

Mole is tremendously interested and excited and follows him (Toad) eagerly up the steps and into the interior of the caravan. The Rat only snorts and thrusts his hands deep into his pockets, remaining where he is.

6. What brings the trip in the yellow cart to an end?

The old grey horse pulling the cart rears up and plunges backwards into a deep ditch, causing the cart to crash and be irredeemably wrecked.

7. At the end of the chapter, what item has Toad determined he must have?

Toad now wants a motor-car.

SOCRATIC DISCUSSION QUESTIONS (LOGIC | Dialectic)

1. Contrast the river with the open road — Ratty's version of the good life versus Toad's.

   The river seems to be alive in that it moves along on its own and moves with it all who venture

   into it. The road requires more effort from those who travel on it, for it is hard and dusty,

   while the river is cool and clean. The road requires the traveler to make decisions about

   where he will go, while the river goes where it will. Toad refers to the road as interesting and

   exciting and the river as dull and fusty, while Rat finds the river cozy. Rat finds the river to be a

   companion, while Toad sees the road as something to master.

2. Contrast Toad's version of travel with the canary-colored cart and with the motor-car. How has Toad's vision of the open road changed? Use a quote from the text to support your answer.

   Toad sees the cart as a pleasant way to enjoy the sights and sounds of the open road. He

   says, "The whole world before you, and a horizon that's always changing!" When he sees the

   motor-car, he falls in love with the sights and sounds of the car itself. He no longer cares about

   enjoying the open road. Instead, Toad envisions dust-clouds springing up behind him as he

   speeds on his reckless way, flinging carts carelessly into the ditch.

3. What is an epiphany? Who has one? When?

   An epiphany is a moment of sudden realization; Toad has an epiphany when he sees the

   motor-car and realizes it is the only means of transportation for him.

Chapter 3

READING NOTES

1. **siesta** – a nap

2. **golden guineas** – British coins

3. **hummocks** – very small, rounded hills; knolls

WORDS TO BE DEFINED

> ### Definitions Bank
>
> a feeling of sorrow for wrongdoing
>
> enthusiasm; excited energy
>
> green
>
> in a childish, bad-tempered way
>
> to be kindly accommodating
>
> unbelieving
>
> weary; weak

1. They recalled the **languorous** siesta of hot midday

   weary; weak

2. he wandered by the **verdant** banks of dream-rivers

   green

3. "Really, Rat," said the Mole quite **pettishly**

   in a childish, bad-tempered way

4. The Rat attacked a snow-bank beside them with **ardour**

   enthusiasm; excited energy

5. more to **oblige** the Rat than for any other reason

   to be kindly accommodating

6. the astonished and hitherto **incredulous** Mole

   unbelieving

7. "Rat!" he cried in **penitence**, "you're a wonder!"

   a feeling of sorrow for wrongdoing

📖 *Read Chapter 3, marking the text in key places according to the method taught in "How to Mark a Book."*

COMPREHENSION QUESTIONS

1. Who does Mole determine he wants to meet in Chapter 3?

   Mole wants to make the acquaintance of Badger.

2. Give two examples from the beginning of the chapter where Mole acts childishly.

   Mole pesters Rat about taking him to meet Badger; Mole sneaks out into the Wild Wood after

   Rat has warned him about going there.

3. List the "scary" things that Mole experiences as he walks through the Wild Wood.

   Mole is frightened by fungi on the stumps that seem to be making faces at him, by faces

   of animals looking out at him from holes in the woods, and by the strange whistling and

   pattering sounds.

4. How does Ratty find Mole, and where is he?

   Ratty first sees Mole's boot prints heading toward the Wild Wood. He then goes into the

   woods and calls for Mole throughout the wood until he hears Mole call back from a hollow,

   exhausted and trembling.

5. After Mole takes a rest, what new development adds to the difficulty of the pair finding their way home?

   After Mole's rest, Ratty pokes his head out of the stump to find that it is snowing hard.

6. What are the three clues Ratty uses to find Badger's home?

   The first clue is the door-scraper upon which Mole has cut his leg. The second clue is a door-

   mat, and the third clue is the door itself with an iron bell-pull and a brass plate engraved with

   the name of Mr. Badger.

SOCRATIC DISCUSSION QUESTIONS (LOGIC | Dialectic)

Reread the following passages and answer the questions:

1. *Such a rich chapter it had been, when one came to look back on it all! With illustrations so numerous and so very highly colored! The pageant of the river bank had marched steadily along, unfolding itself in scene-pictures that succeeded each other in stately procession. Purple loosestrife arrived early, shaking luxuriant tangled locks along the edge of the mirror whence its own face laughed back at it. Willow-herb, tender and wistful, like a pink sunset cloud was not slow to follow. Comfrey, the purple hand-in-hand with the white, crept forth to take its place in the line; and at last one morning the <u>diffident and delaying dog-rose stepped delicately on the stage</u>, and one knew, as if string music had announced it in stately chords that strayed into a gavotte, that June at last was here.*

    a. Explain the two metaphors Grahame uses in this passage.

        Grahame compares the changing seasons to chapters in a book. He also compares the

        blooming of nature in spring to that of a river bank marching in a pageant.

    b. Explain how Grahame uses nature to express the passing of time.

        Grahame uses the succession of blooming plants and trees to mark the passing of time.

    c. What are the examples of personification evident in this passage?

        Examples of personification include: purple loosestrife shaking tangled locks, comfrey

        crept forth in the line, and the dog-rose stepped on the stage.

    d. Underline the alliteration in the passage.

2.	*It was a cold still afternoon with a hard steely sky overhead, when he slipped out of the warm parlor into the open air. The country lay bare and entirely leafless around him, and he thought that he had never seen so far and so intimately into the insides of things as on that winter day when Nature was deep in her annual slumber and seemed to have kicked the clothes off. Copses, dells, quarries and all hidden places, which had been mysterious mines for exploration in leafy summer, now exposed themselves and their secrets pathetically, and seemed to ask him to overlook their shabby poverty for a while, till they could riot in rich masquerade as before, and trick and entice him with the old deceptions. It was pitiful in a way, and yet cheering — even exhilarating. He was glad that he liked the country undecorated, hard, and stripped of its finery. He had got down to the bare bones of it, and they were fine and strong and simple. He did not want the warm clover and the play of seeding grasses; the screens of quickset, the billowy drapery of beech and elm seemed best away; and with great cheerfulness of spirit he pushed on towards the Wild Wood, which lay before him low and threatening, like a black reef in some still southern sea.*

a.	Explain the difference in the winter landscape and the summer landscape.

The winter landscape is bare and leafless, allowing Mole to see into all the hidden places

the summer foliage had kept hidden. The winter is shabby, poor, and exposed, while the

summer was rich with color and finery.

b.	Why does Mole prefer the winter landscape over the summer landscape?

Mole prefers the winter landscape because it is undecorated, and he can see "the bare

bones of it." He does not care for the mystery of what lies behind all the greenery.

c.	At the end of the passage, Grahame's tone toward the landscape shifts, foreshadowing trouble ahead. What words does he use to signify this, and what might this suggest?

At the end of the passage, Grahame uses the landscape to foreshadow trouble. He

compares the Wild Wood to a low and threatening black reef in a southern sea.

3. *"You shouldn't really have gone and done it, Mole. I did my best to keep you from it. We river-bankers, we hardly ever come here by ourselves. If we have to come, we come in couples, at least; then we're generally all right. Besides, there are a hundred things one has to know, which we understand all about and you don't, as yet. I mean passwords, and signs, and sayings which have power and effect, and plants you carry in your pocket, and verses you repeat, and dodges and tricks you practice; all simple enough when you know them, but they've got to be known if you're small, or you'll find yourself in trouble. Of course if you were Badger or Otter, it would be quite another matter."*

a. In this passage, Rat is speaking to Mole. He says, "I did my best to keep you from it." What was he trying to "keep" Mole from and why?

Rat was trying to keep him from the dangers and "the Terror of the Wild Wood."

b. Explain how this chapter and specifically this passage reflect the mentor/student or parent/child relationship that has developed between Rat and Mole.

In this chapter, we see Mole act like a child when he does not heed the advice of Rat

to not go into the Wild Wood to meet Badger. Mole becomes "wise in his own eyes"

and goes on the adventure unprepared for the dangers and terror ahead. Rat shows a

parentlike reaction when he realizes the house is empty and that Mole has run off into

certain trouble. Rat arms himself and heads toward the danger to save Mole. When he

finds Mole, he reprimands him as a parent would a child.

c. What message might Grahame be giving his own son through this passage?

The message Grahame seems to be giving his son through this passage is that Grahame

knows what is best for his son and that what Grahame does, he does to protect his son.

He also says that there are a lot of simple lessons that a person needs to learn to be safe

in the world, especially if he is small.

Chapter 4

READING NOTES

1. **oaken settles** – wooden benches with arms, high solid backs, and seats that function as storage

2. **Society** – one's community; a people group sharing common traditions, ideas, and values

3. **hedgehogs** – spiny, nocturnal mammals that roll themselves up when threatened

4. **rooks** – black birds

5. **chap** – fellow

WORDS TO BE DEFINED

Definitions Bank		
agreed	drowsiness; sleepiness	orders
cooler than is comfortable due to air currents	harshness; roughness	threatening
cut out	in a fatherly way	to strike with an open hand
	meal	

1. "This is not the sort of night for small animals to be out," he said **paternally**.

   in a fatherly way _____

2. where he had been busy laying a **repast** _____ meal _____

3. In accordance with the kindly Badger's **injunctions** _____ orders _____

4. comparative or actual **somnolence** _____ drowsiness; sleepiness _____

5. I had to **cuff** his head once or twice _____ to strike with an open hand _____

6. Supposing the rooms are **drafty**

   cooler than is comfortable due to air currents _____

7. The Mole **assented** heartily _____ agreed _____

8. a damp and airless tunnel, part vaulted, part rock

   cut out _____

9. the whole mass of the Wild Wood, dense, **menacing**, compact _____ threatening _____

10. For others the **asperities** _____ harshness; roughness _____

📖 *Read Chapter 4, marking the text in key places according to the method taught in "How to Mark a Book."*

COMPREHENSION QUESTIONS

1. What three forms of hospitality does Badger show Rat and Mole when they first arrive?

    Badger first shows hospitality by setting Mole and Rat by the fire to warm themselves and

    giving them dry dressing gowns. Next, he cleans up Mole's shin. Finally, he lays out a meal

    for them.

2. When conversation finally begins, who does Badger ask about first and what news is given?

    When conversation begins, Badger first asks about Toad. Badger learns that Toad is a reckless

    driver and has had seven smashes. Toad has already been in the hospital three times and has

    had to pay numerous fines.

3. What fear does Rat have for Toad's fate?

    Rat fears that Toad will either be "killed or ruined."

4. The next morning, Mole and Rat find hedgehogs at the breakfast table. Where do they say Badger is, and what do they say he is doing? What is Badger really doing?

    The hedgehogs say that Badger is in his study and that he is particularly busy and should not

    be disturbed. Badger is actually napping.

5. What do Badger and Mole find they have in common?

    Badger and Mole learn that they both have an appreciation for underground living.

6. What does Badger teach Mole about the history of the Wild Wood?

Badger teaches Mole that there were badgers that lived in that place long ago, but then the
humans came and built a strong city. After that, the humans left for no clear reason. The city
fell to ruins over time and the badgers came back, as did the trees and plants. The trees and
plants developed in the Wild Wood, and all the animals began to move back. Badger says that
someday the humans may even come back again, but no one worries about that. He says that
it takes all sorts to make a world.

SOCRATIC DISCUSSION QUESTIONS (LOGIC | Dialectic)

1. When Badger answers the door to find Ratty and Mole in the Wild Wood in the snow at
that hour of night, what does Badger's reaction suggest about his relationship with Rat?
What evidence from the text supports this?

When Badger sees that it is Ratty, he lets them in and admonishes them for being out in the
Wild Wood at that late hour. Badger pats both of their heads. "This is not the sort of night
for small animals to be out," he said paternally. The pat on the head and the admonishment
suggest that Badger is older and wiser. Badger places himself above both animals in doing
this. Grahame says that Badger speaks paternally to Rat, suggesting that he has parented
or mentored Rat. Badger invites the pair into his kitchen where there is a fire and supper,
showing his care and compassion for the animals.

2. Beginning on the second page of the chapter, Grahame uses personification multiple times
when describing Badger's kitchen. Find and list at least three examples. What do these
phrases suggest about the mood in Badger's kitchen?

Examples of personification include: "Rows of spotless plates winked," "The ruddy brick
floor smiled up," "the oaken settles ... exchanged cheerful glances with each other," "plates
... grinned at pots," and "the merry firelight flickered and played." The phrases suggest an
inviting and welcoming setting.

3. Grahame uses the underground to represent the inner self, the mind and heart of a person. Find and reread the passage where Mole begins to tell Badger about being underground. What are the benefits of the underground, according to Mole and Badger, and how does this relate to what you know about your own inner self?

Mole says that in the underground "you know exactly where you are. Nothing can happen to you, and nothing can get at you. You're entirely your own master, and you don't have to consult anybody or mind what they say. Things go on all the same overhead, and you let 'em, and don't bother about 'em. When you want to, up you go, and there the things are, waiting for you." Badger agrees and adds, "There's no security, or peace and tranquillity, except underground. And then, if your ideas get larger and you want to expand—why, a dig and a scrape, and there you are!" He also says that there is no one to judge you or make remarks about you. This relates to the inner self because you are free to think whatever you want in your own head; there is no one to judge your thoughts. You can imagine as much or as little as you like without anyone to remark on your thoughts. It is a safe space.

4. Reread the last paragraph of Chapter 4. "Know thyself" is an often-repeated maxim. What does Moles realize about himself? How does this show growth in character?

By the end of Chapter 4, Mole begins to understand his place in the world. He realizes, "clearly that he was an animal of tilled field and hedgerow, linked to the ploughed furrow, the frequented pasture, the lane of evening lingerings, the cultivated garden-plot." He knows he does not belong in the rough parts of Nature; rather, he belongs in "the pleasant places in which his lines were laid and which held adventure enough." This shows that Mole has grown in character. He has ventured into new places and now sees clearly where he belongs.

RHETORIC | Expression

The student expresses in his or her own words the Central One Idea with supporting details.

❶ CENTRAL ONE IDEA

1. In a paragraph, **summarize** Chapters 1-4.

    Answers will vary. Here is an example:

    In Chapter 1, Mole discovers the world above the ground, where he meets and befriends

    many other animals, such as Rat, who teaches him to boat and enjoy the water. He comes

    to love being above ground, and he and Rat spend lots of time on the water and exploring

    the outdoors. After time passes, in Chapter 2, Rat introduces Mole and Toad, and the three

    of them set out on an adventure in Toad's caravan, until it is run off the road by a motor-car.

    Their hopes for adventure are ruined, and they return home again. Winter comes in Chapter 3;

    Toad now loves cars, and Mole is determined to meet Badger. He sets out on his own into the

    new and scary Wild Wood, but gets stuck along the way. Rat comes to his rescue, but they get

    stuck in a snowstorm and find shelter in Badger's home on the edge of the Wild Wood. Finally,

    in Chapter 4, Rat and Mole stay with Badger and relax in his home until Otter comes and leads

    them back home where Mole is happiest to be.

2. Write the **Central One Idea** of Chapters 1-4 in a complete sentence.

    Answers will vary.

3. List three or four points that support your determination of the Central One Idea.

    Answers will vary. Support for the Teacher's Central One Idea: (1) Mole pushes through to the outer world,

    having never experienced it before. Everything is new and exciting to him, and he is not sure where to go

    or what to do. (2) After acting foolishly on the boat and needing rescue, Rat asks Mole to stay with him and

    let him teach him about life on the river. (3) After the cart accident, Mole and Rat help Toad clean up the

    wreckage and get him back home safely. (4) Ratty explains his experience of the river bank, Wild Wood, and

    Wide World to Mole. (5) Ratty teaches Mole how to put together the clues. (6) Badger explains the history

    of the Wild Wood to Mole and also explains his own place in it.

❶ CENTRAL ONE IDEA (as expressed by the teacher)

All people need trusted friends and mentors to guide them and help them to understand the

world, society, and their place in both.

ESSAY OPTION

1. **Guided Essay:** Mole is introduced to the reader in the spring season. Write an essay on the characteristics of spring and how this is representative of Mole's character. Use examples from the book to support your idea.

2. **Independent Essay:** Just as Mole is introduced in spring, the season he represents, the reader meets Badger in winter. Write an essay comparing the winter season to the winter season of life. How does this season reflect Badger's character? Use evidence from the text to support your answer.

Student Essay:
(A good essay length is between 2-3 pages.)

Guided Essay:

1. Have students share their thoughts on spring. Ask what things come to mind. List these for the students. (Examples might include: newness/freshness; green shoots pushing through the ground; tender foliage not yet bloomed; things not yet fully developed; bright sunny skies; warmer temperatures; the excitement of things growing and changing.)

2. Have students list characteristics of Mole and lead them to compare this list to the list about spring. Discuss how as humans we have seasons of life. Spring represents youth and innocence, a time to learn and grow. In youth, we are dependent on others to teach us.

3. Have students find and list passages that support Mole being young and in the spring season of life and needing to be taught.

4. Help students develop an outline for their essay.

5. Help students develop a topic sentence for the essay, using words from the question in their statement. **Example:** Having lived underground all his life, Mole feels the upward pull of spring and digs through the ground to pop out on the surface like a tulip bulb on the first warm day after winter.

Independent Essay:

1. Winter: Winter is bare, cold, and without the pageantry of the other seasons. It is the final season of the year. Winter is quiet and slower.

2. Badger: He is in his senior years; he is not concerned anymore with social conventions and their pageantry; he speaks plainly and to the point. Badger moves more slowly and often naps.

PART TWO

Chapters 5-9

PRE-GRAMMAR | Preparation

Prepare the student for understanding the Central One Idea
by drawing upon his or her prior knowledge or experience.

1. Think of a time when you have been away from home for a period of time (vacation, camp, sleepover, or even a very long day of running errands). Briefly describe how it feels to return home.

    _____

    _____

    _____

    _____

    _____

    _____

2. Think of a time when someone was trying to help you, but you did not want his help or advice. How did you treat him? What was the result of not taking his advice?

    _____

    _____

    _____

    _____

    _____

    _____

3. Can you think of a time when you felt led by God to take action? What did He call you to do? Did you act upon His call? What was the result?

    _____

    _____

    _____

    _____

    _____

GRAMMAR | Presentation
LOGIC | Dialectic

In the Grammar section, the student is presented with and discovers essential facts, elements, and features of the novel. In the Logic section, the student reasons with the facts, elements, and features of the novel; invents, sorts, arranges, compares, and connects ideas—and begins to uncover and determine the Central One Idea.

Chapter 5

READING NOTES

1. *Dulce Domum* – Latin for "Sweet Home"

2. **skittle** – a game similar to bowling

3. **Capital!** – an exclamation meaning "Great!"

4. *pate de foie gras* – goose liver pate—an expensive delicacy

5. **mulled ale** – hot, spiced beer (cooked in a pot much like spiced cider)

WORDS TO BE DEFINED

> ## Definitions Bank
>
> | | |
> |---|---|
> | accessory | overbearing |
> | a short humorous or interesting story | poor; scanty |
> | | sorrowfully; mournfully |
> | food; provisions | sudden outburst |
> | off and on, rather than continuous | torn in two |
> | | to talk too much |

1. every wire, perch, and **appurtenance** distinct and recognizable

   accessory

2. Poor Mole stood alone in the road, his heart torn **asunder**

   torn in two

3. astonished and dismayed at the violence of Mole's **paroxysm** of grief

   sudden outburst

4. sniffs were frequent and sobs only **intermittent**

   off and on, rather than continuous

5. dragged back along the road by his **imperious** companion

   overbearing

6. who by a flow of cheerful talk and **anecdote** endeavoured to beguile his spirits back

   a short humorous or interesting story

7. its narrow, **meager** dimensions, its worn and shabby contents

   poor; scanty

8. "No bread!" groaned the Mole **dolorously**

   sorrowfully; mournfully

9. show off their points to his visitor, and **expatiate** on them

   to talk too much

10. on the **provender** so magically provided

   food; provisions

📖 *Read Chapter 5, marking the text in key places according to the method taught in "How to Mark a Book."*

COMPREHENSION QUESTIONS

1. What have Mole and Ratty been doing when this chapter opens? Who was with them?

   Mole and Ratty have been on a long day's outing exploring and hunting the wide uplands.

   They were with Otter.

2. Why do they decide to go through the village instead of sticking to the animal paths?

   They decide to cut through the village because the humans in the village are indoors by this time

   and the animals can slip through safely and peek in at the people through their windows.

3. One of the major themes of *The Wind in the Willows* is friendship. Ratty proves himself to be a great friend to Mole once again. List the ways that Ratty supports and encourages Mole in the chapter.

   • Ratty notices Mole is not himself and offers to let him rest.

   • He asks Mole to tell him his troubles so he can try and help.

   • He pats Mole gently on the shoulder when Mole expresses his frustration.

   • He calls himself a "pig" and insists on finding Mole's home.

   • He works to make Mole's home clean and inviting and encourages Mole to do the same.

   • He encourages Mole to tell him the stories about his home and the things in it.

   • He sends a field-mouse out with money to get supplies to serve the carolers.

   • He takes care of Mole's guests so that Mole can relax and enjoy their company.

4. According to the carolers, who was the first to cry "Nowell"?

   The animals were the first to cry "Nowell."

SOCRATIC DISCUSSION QUESTIONS (LOGIC | Dialectic)

1. In Chapter 5, Grahame shows the importance of being connected to your roots through Mole's character. Find and reread the paragraph that starts with "Home! That was what they meant." How does Mole describe his home? Why does he want to go see his home even though he does not describe it as anything special?

   Mole describes his home as "Shabby indeed, and small and poorly furnished." However, he

   wants to see it because he says it is, "the home he had made for himself, the home he had

   been so happy to get back to after his day's work. And the home had been happy with him,

   too." This is the place that Mole had created for himself, and he had many wonderful and

   comfortable memories there; while it was not grand, it was his and it was special to him.

2. Though Mole's heart is described as being "torn asunder" when Ratty does not stop at Mole's request to visit Mole's old home, Grahame writes, "But even under such a test as this his [Mole's] loyalty to his friend stood firm. Never for a moment did he dream of abandoning him." Why is Mole willing to follow Ratty, though he so desperately wants to visit his old home? What is Grahame suggesting about friendship in this paragraph?

   Mole, though in anguish, follows Ratty because he is a loyal friend. Grahame is demonstrating

   the importance of sacrifice people make for those they care about. Ratty has been good to

   Mole, and Mole is willing to sacrifice his desires to stay with his friend.

3. Ultimately, Mole has a major growth of character at the end of this chapter. By going home again, what has Mole learned about himself and where he belongs? What does Grahame mean by "the special value of some such anchorage in one's existence"?

By the end of the chapter, Mole has discovered that while he loves his old home, he has

outgrown it. He realizes that he wants to be in the larger outer world. No matter how small or

humble his beginnings, he is glad he has the old place to revisit and relive some of the good

memories. He realizes that he cannot and does not want to stay in the memories forever.

Grahame is showing that our memories are our anchorage in the world. They remind us who

we are and where we have come from. They can give us strength to get through troubled

times, but are not a place to remain forever.

Chapter 6

1. **gaiters** – leg coverings

2. **gauntleted gloves** – protective or dress gloves extending above the wrist

3. **Red Lion** – the inn where Toad is eating when he sees the motor-car and steals it

4. **Chairman of the Bench of Magistrates** – the chief judge of the district

5. **Clerk** – government official responsible for keeping records and accounts

6. **cheeking** – talking back; sassing

7. **gaoler** – jailer

WORDS TO BE DEFINED

> ### Definitions Bank
>
> ashamed
>
> clothing for a specific kind of occasion
>
> crouching or shrinking away in fear
>
> dressing up
>
> faces or facial expressions
>
> incapable of being corrected or reformed
>
> insulting, irreverent, or defiant speech or conduct
>
> magnificent and impressive clothing
>
> sarcastic; hurtful
>
> wavered; weakened

1. Toad is busily **arraying** himself in those singularly hideous habiliments so dear to him

   dressing up

2. Toad is busily arraying himself in those singularly hideous **habiliments** so dear to him

   clothing for a specific kind of occasion

3. His hearty accents **faltered** and fell away

   wavered; weakened

4. the stern unbending look on the **countenances** of his silent friends

   faces or facial expressions

5. seemed to have evaporated with the removal of his fine **panoply**

   magnificent and impressive clothing

6. Badger's **caustic**, not to say brutal, remarks

    sarcastic; hurtful

7. "He did it awfully well," said the **crestfallen** Rat.

    ashamed

8. the **incorrigible** rogue and hardened ruffian

    incapable of being corrected or reformed

9. whom we see **cowering** in the dock before us

    crouching or shrinking away in fear

10. gross **impertinence** to the rural police

    insulting, irreverent, or defiant speech or conduct

📖 *Read Chapter 6, marking the text in key places according to the method taught in "How to Mark a Book."*

COMPREHENSION QUESTIONS

1. What season is it when this chapter opens?

    When Chapter 6 opens, it is the early part of the summer.

2. When Badger arrives at Ratty's home, what announcement does he make?

    Badger announces, "The hour has come! ... The hour of Toad!" He has come to help Ratty and

    Mole make Toad a sensible animal.

3. When Toad finds himself locked in his room and unable to be the "Terror of the Highway," what does he do at first to pass the time?

    When Toad finds himself locked in his room, he arranges the furniture into a shape that

    resembles a motor-car, gets in, and drives while making road noises, until the end when he

    turns a complete somersault and lies amidst the ruins.

4. What warning does the Badger give Rat when Rat takes over the watch of Toad?

When Rat comes for his shift, Badger warns him that when Toad is quiet and submissive, that

is when he is at his "artfullest" and is sure to be up to something.

5. How does Toad make his escape, and what sin does he bask in as he walks down the road?

After convincing Rat to go find help such as a doctor or lawyer, Toad ties together the

bedsheets to shimmy out of the window. As he walks down the street, Toad revels in the sin

of pride. Grahame writes about Toad that, "all nature joining in a chorus of approval to the

song of self-praise that his own heart was singing to him, he almost danced along the road in

his satisfaction and conceit."

6. Toad's descent into crime does not happen with one willful decision, but in a series of steps. What were the steps?

Toad's descent into crime starts when he allows himself to just look at the motor-car.

"There cannot be any harm in my only looking at it!" he says. He then walks slowly around it,

inspecting, criticizing, and musing deeply. He fixates on the car. He then decides to engage the

car. He starts the engine. With sight, hearing, and mind possessed, he loses self-control and

finds himself in the car turning the wheel. Grahame writes, "the old passion seized on Toad

and completely mastered him, body and soul."

7. Toward the end of the chapter, there is a dramatic scene change. Where is Toad now? Why do you think Grahame did not start with an indented paragraph?

Toward the end of the chapter, Toad is in a courtroom being charged with crimes. The

paragraph is not indented because the reader is entering mid-scene. The reader is not taken

through the entire scene of the self-destruction of Toad, but is moved forward in time to see

Toad's punishment for his lack of self-control.

8. List the crimes Toad is being held accountable for and the number of years he will serve for committing them?

   Toad is found guilty of three crimes: stealing a valuable motor-car (twelve months), driving to

   the public danger (three years), and gross impertinence to the rural police (fifteen years). In

   total, it is rounded up to twenty years.

SOCRATIC DISCUSSION QUESTIONS (LOGIC | Dialectic)

1. By what authority do Badger, Rat, and Mole take Toad "in hand"? What does Badger say that explains why they have come? When are we called to act on behalf of another person? Toad has the money to keep buying cars when he has smashed them. Why can he not do as he pleases?

   Badger, Rat, and Mole take Toad "in hand" by the authority of friendship and the animal

   community's expectations. Badger says, "we animals never allow our friends to make fools of

   themselves beyond a certain limit; and that limit you've reached." As a society, we are called to

   intervene when someone is at risk of harming themselves or someone else. While Toad might have

   the money to continue to buy more cars, his driving is a danger to himself and the public.

2. Think of a time when you have given into temptation. Did it happen all at once, or did it come in small stages that led to the sin? We can learn much about ourselves and others by reading about the experiences of characters in literature, even if they are animals. Toad illustrates a universal human weakness that we all have to some degree. What is the weakness? What could Toad have done that might have prevented him from landing in jail?

   Answers will vary. (An example to help illustrate: A person is on a diet to improve his health.

   There is a pan of brownies on the kitchen counter. At first, the person says, "I will just smell

   them; there is no harm in that." This leads to, "I will just taste a crumb—that cannot harm

   anything." Before even realizing it, he has eaten half the pan.) The weakness Toad illustrates

   is a lack of self-control for something that he covets. Toad should have stayed away from the

   temptation altogether. He should not have walked out to the parking lot, because that was

   putting himself in a place for the sin to occur.

3. Grahame, as the author, determines the length of punishment Toad receives for his guilty actions. While stealing the car was the worst offense, why did "cheeking" get the most severe punishment? What message about Toad's choices during his self-destruction might Grahame have been sending to his own son through this passage?

   Grahame seems to understand that humans are weak and will make sinful choices when

   tempted. He shows that those choices come with consequences. For example, Toad

   stole the motor-car and received punishment for this, but "cheeking" resulted in a more

   serious consequence. Grahame is sending a message to his son that though mistakes carry

   consequences, they will be far worse if one talks back to those in authority rather than

   showing remorse for wrongdoing.

Chapter 7

READING NOTES

1. **Little Portly** – Otter's young son
2. **ford** – shallow body of water that can be crossed by wading
3. **reeds and bulrushes** – grasslike plants growing in shallow water or marshy ground
4. **osiers** – willow trees
5. **Pan** – in Greek mythology, the god of woods, field, and flock, having a human torso and head with goat legs, horns, and ears
6. **pan-pipes** – a series of short pipes bound together in graduated lengths with the mouthpieces in an even row, named after the god Pan

WORDS TO BE DEFINED

> ### Definitions Bank
>
> constantly changing; unpredictable
>
> decorated as with jewels
>
> deserving of reverence
>
> edge growth
>
> rest
>
> scorching hot
>
> short pleasure journey; an outing
>
> soon-coming
>
> total forgetfulness

1. the dark **selvedge** of the river bank

   edge growth

2. the sullen heats of the **torrid** afternoon broke up and rolled away

   scorching hot

3. plying their trades and vocations through the night till sunshine should fall on them at last and send them off to their well-earned **repose**

   rest

4. the color of the flowers that **gemmed** the water's edge

   decorated as with jewels

5. some **august** Presence was very, very near

   deserving of reverence

6. in the utter clearness of the **imminent** dawn

   soon-coming

7. a **capricious** little breeze, dancing up from the surface of the water

   constantly changing; unpredictable

8. and with its soft touch came instant **oblivion**

   total forgetfulness

9. a **jaunt** on the river

   short pleasure journey; an outing

📖 *Read Chapter 7, marking the text in key places according to the method taught in "How to Mark a Book."*

COMPREHENSION QUESTIONS

1. What is Mole doing at the opening of the chapter? What is the setting?

    At the opening of the chapter, Mole lies stretched on the river bank, trying to cool down after

    a hot summer day. It is late in the evening, after 10 p.m., but there is still some lingering light

    from the departed day. The heat is just beginning to lift.

2. Ratty once again shows his ability to make keen observations. What is he able to discern about Otter's behavior? What does he learn?

    Ratty is able to discern that Otter is really worried about Little Portly. Though he knows Portly

    often wanders off at times, Otter is concerned about the length of time that he has been gone

    this time. Ratty also learns that Little Portly is not a strong swimmer.

3. Where does Otter go every night in hopes of finding Portly? Why does he choose that spot?

    Otter returns to the old ford. He goes there because that was where he taught Portly to swim,

    and Portly liked that spot. He hopes that Portly will recognize the spot if he comes wandering

    through and will remember it and play there for a while.

4. As Mole and Rat search for Portly, who first hears music? How does it make him feel when the music goes away?

    Rat is first to hear the beautiful music and guides Mole to steer the boat in the direction it

    came from. When he loses the sound of the music for a moment, Rat sinks into his chair and

    says that it was so beautiful, strange, and new that he wishes he had not ever heard it because

    it has left him feeling empty and nothing seems to compare to it.

5. Where does the music lead Rat and Mole? Who do they find there?

The music leads them to the place of Ratty's song-dream, a holy place. When they get there,

they see Pan and Little Portly.

6. At the end of the chapter, what is revealed about Pan in his song?

Pan reveals that if an animal should find himself in trouble or need, he will be there to help—

but the animal will not remember the encounter. Pan calls himself a helper and healer.

SOCRATIC DISCUSSION QUESTIONS (LOGIC | Dialectic)

1. Though he does not directly say it, what does Ratty imply might have happened to Little Portly? What lines from the text support this?

Ratty fears that Little Portly has died. He thinks he may have drowned or been caught in a

trap. Otter has told him that Little Portly is not a good swimmer and that he has been missing

for days, with no traces of him anywhere. There is also a lot of water coming down the weir—

a place Little Portly loves. A supporting line that shows Ratty thinks Little Portly may have died

is, "The child loved the spot, and Otter thinks that if he came wandering back from wherever

he is—if he *is* anywhere by this time, poor little chap—he might make for the ford he was so

fond of."

2. When Mole and Rat go looking for Little Portly, the reader learns that Mole is steering the boat. How is this different from Chapter 1? What does this suggest about Mole's character?

In the first chapter, Mole did not know how to row a boat; when he grabbed the oars from Ratty,

he ended up flipping the boat and needing to be rescued. Now Mole is rowing the boat. This

shows growth in Mole's character. He has been learning lessons and is able to apply them. Ratty is

beginning to trust Mole with greater responsibilities.

3. When Pan gives the animals who have been in his presence "oblivion," he calls it a gift. Why is this a gift? What would happen if he did not wipe their memories of encountering him?

Pan gives the animals he helps oblivion because he knows the power and awe they will feel

with him and the feeling that nothing else can compare when he leaves them. He gives them

oblivion so that they can continue to experience joy and happiness once he is gone. If he did

not wipe their memories, they would be depressed and long to be with him.

4. Compare how Mole and Ratty feel in the presence of Pan to how Toad feels in the presence of a motor-car. In likening Pan to God, what is Grahame suggesting about the difference between answering the call of God and the call of self-desire?

Mole, Rat, and Toad are all called by a sound. Mole and Rat hear the music of Pan and Toad the

"poop-poop" of the motor-car. Each of the animals is entranced by and drawn to the sounds.

When Mole and Rat come before Pan, they feel "wonderfully at peace and happy." They are

awed and bow their heads and worship. This ultimately results in them finding Little Portly and

returning him home to his father. When Toad was in the presence of the motor-car, he gave

in to his own selfish desires, which caused him to commit several crimes and landed him in

prison with a twenty-year sentence. Grahame seems to suggest that following the call of God

leads to good, while following the call of selfish desires leads to ruin.

Chapter 8

READING NOTES

1. **bubble-and-squeak** – a British comfort food of boiled cabbage and potatoes fried together

2. **gaoler's daughter** – the jailer's daughter, who pities Toad and wants to take care of him

3. **coach-and-four** – a fancy coach drawn by four horses

4. **golden sovereigns** – gold coins with about the same value as the British pound

WORDS TO BE DEFINED

Definitions Bank

a common girl or young woman	enclosed; entombed
a condition specified in an agreement	lacking in seriousness
a cover to protect the back or arms of furniture	outgoing; confidently optimistic
amusing by pretending	recklessly bold
characterized by friendliness	witty remarks

1. Toad found himself **immured** in a dank and noisome dungeon ____enclosed; entombed____

2. **disporting** himself as if he had bought up every road in England
   ____amusing by pretending____

3. in such an **audacious** manner ____recklessly bold____

4. a pleasant **wench** ____a common girl or young woman____

5. shrouded in an **antimacassar** on the parlor table
   ____a cover to protect the back or arms of furniture____

6. Toad was very much the same **sanguine**, self-satisfied animal
   ____outgoing; confidently optimistic____

7. "There, there," said Toad graciously and **affably** ____characterized by friendliness____

8. the only **stipulation** the old lady made being that she should be gagged
   ____a condition specified in an agreement____

9. The chaff and the humorous **sallies** to which he was subjected ____witty remarks____

10. Toad ceased his **frivolous** antics ____lacking in seriousness____

📖 *Read Chapter 8, marking the text in key places according to the method taught in "How to Mark a Book."*

COMPREHENSION QUESTIONS

1. What feelings does Toad express about himself and his friends in his first few weeks of being in jail?

    In the first few weeks of his prison sentence, Toad is in despair and shedding bitter tears. He

    laments his old life and how handsome, rich, and carefree he was. He admits that he was a

    stupid animal, while his friends were wise, intelligent, and sensible.

2. The gaoler's daughter has pity on Toad. Why does she want to help Toad?

    The gaoler's daughter wants to help Toad because she is fond of animals and she wants to

    teach him to eat from her hand and sit up and do all sorts of tricks.

3. How does the gaoler's daughter view her relationship with Toad? How does Toad perceive how she feels about him, and what does he see as the problem between them?

    The gaoler's daughter views Toad as a pet. She takes pity on him. Toad's vanity allows him to

    believe her interest in him comes from a "growing tenderness" and that she "admired him

    very much."

4. What does the gaoler's daughter list as Toad's chief fault? What is one of his virtues?

    The gaoler's daughter declares that Toad's chief fault is that he talks too much. His virtue,

    however, is his honesty to admit when he is wrong.

5. The gaoler's daughter develops a plan for Toad's escape. What are the terms of the plan?

The plan is for Toad to pay the washerwoman to trade clothes with him so that he can disguise

himself as the washerwoman and walk out of the prison. The washerwoman is to be bound

and gagged so that it looks like she had nothing to do with the plan.

6. Where does Toad go first after escaping prison, and what problem does he encounter when he gets there?

After escaping prison, Toad heads for the train station. However, when he gets there, he

realizes he is not in his own clothes and has no money for a ticket.

7. How is Toad able to secure a ride from the engine-driver of the train?

Toad is able to secure a ride from the engine-driver by promising to wash several of the

engine-driver's dirty shirts.

8. What three reasons does the engine-driver give for helping Toad?

Though the police are chasing Toad, the engine-driver says that he will help him because

he does not like motor-cars, he does not like being ordered about by policemen on his own

engine, and the sight of an animal in tears makes him softhearted.

9. What is the engine-driver's plan for helping Toad escape the police chasing him?

The engine-driver's plan is to enter the tunnel and slow the train just as it exits the tunnel,

giving Toad time to jump off and escape into the woods.

SOCRATIC DISCUSSION QUESTIONS (LOGIC | Dialectic)

1. In the beginning of this chapter, Toad is in despair as he serves the first few weeks of his prison sentence. What does the gaoler's daughter do that helps bring Toad out of his despair? How is the situation in this chapter similar to the one in Chapter 5: Dulce Domum? Using support from the text, what two ideas from Chapter 5 is Grahame reinforcing in Chapter 8?

    The gaoler's daughter brings Toad comfort food, bubble-and-squeak, and though he does not

    eat it, the smell begins to lift his spirits and makes him think of meals at Toad Hall. Later, she

    brings him tea and buttered toast and begins to talk to him about Toad Hall. This chapter is

    similar to Chapter 5 because when Mole's spirits were low, Ratty tried to cheer him up, round

    up some food to eat, and have Mole talk about the memories of things he had collected in his

    home. Grahame is reinforcing the importance of having friends to care for you and help you

    through hard times as well as the importance of the "anchorage" of home and memories to

    recollect when your spirits are low.

2. When Toad makes his escape from prison, what two items does he leave in his cell and what things are in them? According to Toad, what is the difference between the many-pocketed animal and a one- or no-pocketed animal? Do you think Toad's many pockets help or hurt his character? Explain your answer.

    When Toad escapes from jail, "To his horror he recollected that he had left both coat and

    waistcoat behind him in his cell, and with them his pocket-book, money, keys, watch, matches,

    pencil-case—all that makes life worth living." A many-pocketed animal is a superior animal,

    educated and "the lord of creation." A one- or no-pocketed animal is a lesser, uneducated

    animal that hops about unequipped for life.

    Answers will vary. Toad's many-pocketed life has allowed him to do as he pleases and, up to this

    point, kept him from experiencing any real consequences. Because of this, he has developed a

    lack of self-control and become bolder in his adventures, leading to crime and prison.

3. Describe the situation and setting that Toad finds himself in at the end of Chapter 8. What are some of the similarities and differences between Toad's night in the woods and Mole's night in the woods in Chapter 3: The Wild Wood?

    At the end of the chapter, Toad is in an unknown wood alone, and it is very late, dark, and

    cold. He is far from friends and home, and he begins to hear strange, unfriendly noises. The

    animals he encounters seem to mock him. This is much like Mole's first venture into the

    Wild Wood. Mole felt alone, heard strange noises, and felt like the animals were mocking

    him. Both animals seek shelter in the hollow of a tree. Mole was scared as he hid and began

    to reflect and understand that Ratty had been trying to protect him from this situation; in

    contrast, Toad is arrogant and prideful toward the mocking animals, and when he seeks

    shelter in the tree, he goes straight into a sound sleep rather than reflecting on what caused

    him to end up in such an awful situation.

4. Extra Credit: In your best cursive, find and write out a recipe for bubble-and-squeak.

    Answers will vary.

Chapter 9

READING NOTES

1. **wayfarers** – people who travel or migrate; drifters

2. **Sea Rat** – an old rat who has traveled much of the world by sea

3. **Constantinople** – the ancient capital of the Byzantine (Eastern Roman) Empire

4. **King Sigurd of Norway** – a Norwegian crusader king

5. **North-Easter** – a coastal or oceanic storm with winds coming out of the northeast

WORDS TO BE DEFINED

Definitions Bank

closed in	in a manner full of desire tinged with sadness
eased	
happy and lighthearted; without a care	unable to be taken back
	urgent or commanding
hopelessly	wine
ideal example	wings or feathers

1. The beat and quiver of impatient **pinions** ___wings or feathers___

2. obedient to the **peremptory** call ___urgent or commanding___

3. He returned somewhat **despondently** to his river again ___hopelessly___

4. suggested the Water Rat **wistfully** ___in a manner full of desire tinged with sadness___

5. somewhat narrow and **circumscribed** ___closed in___

6. an **epitome** of my highly-colored life ___ideal example___

7. his hunger was somewhat **assuaged** ___eased___

8. glowing **vintage** of the South ___wine___

9. now ere the **irrevocable** moment passes ___unable to be taken back___

10. a **blithe some** step forward ___happy and lighthearted; without a care___

📖 *Read Chapter 9, marking the text in key places according to the method taught in "How to Mark a Book."*

COMPREHENSION QUESTIONS

1. How is Water Rat feeling at the opening of the chapter? What is the "feeling in the air" that is contributing to his feelings?

   The Water Rat feels restless and does not know why. The feeling in the air is of change as

   animals are departing south.

2. Grahame uses a metaphor to illustrate the departure of the animals. What comparison does he make?

   Grahame compares the animal departure to Nature's Grand Hotel. He says that the animals

   are like guests in a hotel, packing up, paying, and departing.

3. What are the field-mice and swallows doing?

   They are packing up and making plans to travel south.

4. Water Rat meets a Sea Rat. How is the Sea Rat described?

   Sea Rat is described as "lean and keen-featured, and somewhat bowed at the shoulders;

   his paws were thin and long, his eyes much wrinkled at the corners, and he wore small

   gold earrings in his neatly-set, well-shaped ears. His knitted jersey was of a faded blue, his

   breeches, patched and stained, were based on a blue foundation, and his small belongings

   that he carried were tied up in a blue cotton handkerchief."

5. From where has the Sea Rat just come, and where is he going? What is causing the Sea Rat to travel again?

   The Sea Rat has just spent six months on a farm and is now heading south, following the old

   call back to the old life.

6. The Sea Rat says he is in the coastal trade. What does this mean?

   The Sea Rat does not travel far from land, but from port to port up and down the coast.

7. Ratty offers reasons why the sea life would be hard. What are the reasons he gives? How does the Sea Rat counter each objection?

   First, Ratty suggests that it would be difficult to go months out of sight of land, short on provisions. Sea Rat says that he is in the coastal trade and rarely out of sight of land. Next, Ratty says that he thinks it would be hot and stuffy in the hold. Sea Rat says he stays in the captain's cabin (the nicest cabin on the ship). Last, Ratty says it must be a hard life. The Sea Rat counters with, "For the crew it is," suggesting that he travels on the ship but does not do the hard work the crew does.

8. What does the Sea Rat encourage Water Rat to do? Quote the passage.

   The Sea Rat encourages the Water Rat to go with him. He says, "And you, you will come too, young brother; for the days pass, and never return, and the South still waits for you. Take the Adventure, heed the call, now ere the irrevocable moment passes!"

9. When Ratty returns home to pack up, in what state does Mole find him? What does Mole do to restore his friend to his old self?

   Mole finds Ratty in a trancelike, mechanical state. Mole places himself in front of Rat and drags him inside, throws him down, and holds him. Mole locks him in and hides the satchel. He leaves Ratty to rest and then talks to him about their life and the memories of the upcoming season. Finally, Mole encourages Ratty to write poetry.

SOCRATIC DISCUSSION QUESTIONS (LOGIC | Dialectic)

1. Chapter 9 might be considered Ratty's chapter. What season is it when the chapter opens? How has Grahame used this season as a reflection of the stage of life Ratty is in? What conflict is Ratty struggling with in this chapter?

   The chapter opens in late summer just as fall is about to begin. Grahame uses late summer/

   early fall to show that Ratty is at the stage of life where his youth is behind him, but he is not

   yet old, though he is aware that old age is coming. He is having an internal conflict, a midlife

   crisis, as he tries to decide if he should venture out, make memories, and see more of the

   Wide World while he still can.

2. The Sea Rat says that Ratty's life is no doubt the best life in the world, "if only you are strong enough to lead it!" What does he mean by that?

   The Sea Rat is saying that the countryside is beautiful and truly a great place to live, but he

   does not have the strength to stay in one place for very long. Sea Rat needs to travel and see

   other places.

3. The call of nature or instinct is a major theme in this chapter. How do the swallows explain the call? Use a quote from the book to support your answer. What consequence befell the swallow that tried to stay behind and not listen to the call of nature?

   The swallows explain the call of nature as "stirring within us, a sweet unrest; then back come

   the recollections ... one by one the scents and sounds and names of long-forgotten places

   come gradually back and beckon to us." The swallow that tried to stay behind says it was good

   for a few weeks, but then it became dark and cold and there was no food to be found. When

   he could no longer take it, he had to fly through a storm. He still remembers "the blissful

   feeling of the hot sun again." Now he is "always heeding the call! No, I had had my warning;

   never again did I think of disobedience."

4. When the swallows describe to Ratty the pull of nature to the wonderful place in the south that they will be heading to, Ratty asks, "Why do you ever come back, then, at all?" What reason do the swallows give for their return? Read Ecclesiastes 3:1-8. How do these verses relate to the swallows' answer?

When Ratty questions why the swallows ever return, they respond by saying, "And do you think ...

that the other call is not for us too, in its due season? The call of lush meadow-grass, wet orchards,

warm, insect-haunted ponds ... we shall be homesick once more for quiet water-lilies swaying

on the surface of an English stream." The swallows are trying to explain that there is a time and

season for all things, and they will enjoy each in their due time, which is similar to Ecclesiastes 3:1:

"There is a time for everything, and a season for every activity under the heavens."

5. In Chapter 1, Mole asks Ratty about the Wide World. Ratty responds with, "I've never been there, and I'm never going, nor you either, if you've got any sense at all. Don't ever refer to it again, please." How does Chapter 9 contrast with Ratty's original statement about the Wide World? How does Grahame use the Sea Rat to further the internal conflict Ratty is having in this chapter?

Chapter 9 contrasts with the previous feelings Ratty had of the Wide World, because he hears

the call of the south for the first time. Ratty did not want to discuss the Wide World before.

Now as all the other animals pack up to go, his own restlessness allows him to wonder if he

should go as well. Grahame uses the Sea Rat to further add to Ratty's internal conflict by

having him tell glorious stories of his travels as a coastal mariner. He even encourages Ratty to

join him on his next adventure.

6. Though the chapter focuses on Ratty, growth in Mole is evident at the end. What does Mole do that shows he has learned about friendship? What previous experiences did Mole draw on to help Ratty with his crisis?

At the end of the chapter, Mole sees that Ratty is not himself and takes action to help his

friend. "He dragged him inside, threw him down, and held him." Helping Ratty to a chair, he

locks the door and throws the satchel into a drawer so that Ratty will not be tempted to go.

He gives Ratty time to rest while he works on household matters. He then spends time talking

to Ratty about the joys of the season happening now and the wonderful things to come when

winter is upon them. He knows that poetry will help restore Ratty, so he gives him paper and

time to think, knowing this will improve Ratty's condition. Mole learned how to help a friend

in previous chapters. He learned that when a friend is not in control of himself, to restrain

the friend, remove the temptation, and lock him in his room for his own good. Mole learned

this when the friends locked up Toad, trying to bring him to his senses. He learned that when

a friend is distressed, it is good to attend to household matters for him and then talk to him

about pleasant memories. Mole learned this in Chapter 5 when Ratty helped put his house in

order and then encouraged him to tell Ratty all his good memories of the place to restore his

spirits. And just as Ratty knew that helping Mole serve the field-mice would bring him peace,

Mole knew that Ratty needed to write some lines of poetry to completely recover himself.

7. Extra Credit: Look up the description of the Sea Rat and then draw and color a picture of him.

RHETORIC | Expression

The student expresses in his or her own words the Central One Idea with supporting details.

❶ CENTRAL ONE IDEA

1. In a paragraph, **summarize** Chapters 5-9.

   Answers will vary. Here is an example:

   Chapter 5 begins in winter with Mole and Rat returning from an adventure in a nearby village. Mole sniffs out his home and leads Rat there eventually, and they spruce up the place and invite in carolers for a hearty dinner. Chapter 6 tells of Mole, Rat, and Badger's attempt to come between Toad and his obsession with cars, only for Toad to escape their help and get himself into quite a bit of trouble with the law. In Chapter 7, Mole and Rat help Otter search for his lost son. They find him with the piper/Pan and return him to Otter. Chapter 8 shows readers Toad's prison escape with the help of the gaoler's daughter. He gets away by train, but ends up stranded in the woods away from home. The summer is fading in Chapter 9, and Rat feels the reality of different animals leaving for winter. He meets Sea Rat, who tells Rat of all his adventures at sea. Rat gets enchanted by the stories, but with Mole's help, he comes back to reality and his poetry.

2. Write the **Central One Idea** of Chapters 5-9 in a complete sentence.

   Answers will vary.

3. List three or four points that support your determination of the Central One Idea.

   Answers will vary. Support for the Teacher's Central One Idea: (1) Mole hears the call of his home and his spirits are restored when he visits there. (2) Mole and Rat follow the music of Pan and are helped by him. (3) Ratty feels the pull of migration as the seasons change but is helped by Mole during this time of confusion. (4) Toad does not listen to the advice of his friends and gives into temptation, leading him down a path of personal destruction. He steals the motor-car and ends up in jail.

❶ CENTRAL ONE IDEA (as expressed by the teacher)

Pride, deceit, and a lack of self-control lead to destruction and consequences, but listening to

God and those who care for you will carry you through troubled times.

ESSAY OPTION

1. **Independent Essay:** A major theme in *The Wind in the Willows* is friendship. Write an essay explaining how the friends attempted to help each other in Chapters 5-9. Include how the help was received and the result of the help given.

Student Essay:
(A good essay length is between 2-3 pages.)

Students should write a five-paragraph essay (introduction, three body paragraphs, and

conclusion). Have students cite examples of when help was offered in Chapters 5-9. Compile a

list and have students choose three of the examples to use for the body of their essay.

Examples might include:

- Mole hearing the call of his old home but continuing to follow Ratty.
- Ratty taking Mole to his home despite his desire to get to his own home.
- Ratty helping Mole to spruce up his home and listening to Mole talk about the things he has collected in his home.
- Ratty helping Mole throw an impromptu party.
- Badger coming to help Rat and Mole with Toad.
- Toad trying to be remorseful when his friends confront him and lecture him on his behavior.
- Rat and Mole looking for Portly.
- Mole helping Rat return to his old self when Rat is overcome by the Sea Rat's words.

PART THREE

Chapters 10-12

PRE-GRAMMAR | Preparation

Prepare the student for understanding the Central One Idea
by drawing upon his or her prior knowledge or experience.

1. Think of one of your best friends. What are his/her best qualities? What is a fault or bad habit he/she struggles with? What would your friend say is your chief fault?

    _____

    _____

    _____

    _____

    _____

    _____

2. Good friends come to our aid in a time of need. Can you think of a time when you offered help to someone? What did you do for them? Has someone come to your aid? How did he help you?

    _____

    _____

    _____

    _____

    _____

    _____

GRAMMAR | Presentation
LOGIC | Dialectic

In the Grammar section, the student is presented with and discovers essential facts, elements, and features of the novel. In the Logic section, the student reasons with the facts, elements, and features of the novel; invents, sorts, arranges, compares, and connects ideas — and begins to uncover and determine the Central One Idea.

Chapter 10

READING NOTES

1. **canal** – a man-made waterway used for travel and transportation of goods

2. **barge-woman** – a woman driving a barge who, believing Toad to be a washerwoman, offers him a ride to Toad Hall

3. **gorse and bramble** – spiny or prickly shrubs

4. **gipsy** – a wanderer who buys a horse from Toad

5. **shilling and sixpence** – British coins

6. **Kitchener** – a famous British field marshal, diplomat, and statesman

7. **two gentlemen in the motor-car** – the same two men Toad listened to at the Red Lion before stealing their car

WORDS TO BE DEFINED

> ## Definitions Bank
>
> careful; wise
>
> full of pleasure to the senses
>
> making gestures with
> arms and hands
>
> people who go on brief pleasure
> trips or outings
>
> the process of grooming oneself
>
> to be overly affectionate
> or attentive
>
> to quiet or calm
>
> vulgar women

1. his **toilet** complete _____the process of grooming oneself_____

2. little **hussies**, that's what *I* call 'em! _____vulgar women_____

3. I simply **dote** on it. _____to be overly affectionate or attentive_____

4. its chill was not sufficient to **quell** his proud spirit _____to quiet or calm_____

5. the barge-woman was **gesticulating** wildly _____making gestures with arms and hands_____

6. one complete, **voluptuous**, perfect smell _____full of pleasure to the senses_____

7. he was determined to be **prudent** _____careful; wise_____

8. narrow-minded, grudging, timid **excursionists** _____people who go on brief pleasure trips____ or outings_____

📖 *Read Chapter 10, marking the text in key places according to the method taught in "How to Mark a Book."*

COMPREHENSION QUESTIONS

1. What two things wake Toad at the opening of Chapter 10?

    Toad is awakened by the morning sun and his cold feet.

2. As Toad considers which way he should go, what metaphor does Grahame use to describe the relationship of the rustic road and the canal?

The road and canal are compared to two brothers holding hands and walking together.

3. Why story does Toad tell the barge-woman?

Toad tells the barge-woman that he is in sore trouble because he has had to leave his business and troublesome children at home to find out what is wrong with his married daughter. He tells her he has lost his way and his money.

4. What is Toad's chief fault? How does it get him in trouble again?

Toad's fault is that he talks too much, which he does with the barge-woman. He brags to her about how great his business is and how much he loves doing laundry. This gets him into trouble because the barge-woman has him do her washing.

5. What are the consequences of Toad's cheekiness to the barge-woman after she laughs at him?

After Toad loses his temper and makes cheeky comments, the barge-woman humiliates Toad and throws him in the river.

6. When Toad encounters the gipsy, what two things does Toad want so badly at that moment?

Toad is desperate for money in his pocket and a hearty breakfast.

7. What deal does Toad make with the gipsy?

Toad sells the horse to the gipsy for six shillings and sixpence as well as for all he can possibly eat at one sitting from the gipsy's iron pot.

8. What causes Toad to become puffed up and conceited?

   Toad becomes conceited when he thinks of his adventures, his escapes, and the way he has

   outsmarted everyone. His pride begins "to swell within him."

9. While on his journey home, Toad flags down a motor-car in which he hopes to drive up to Toad Hall. What causes Toad to panic as the car gets closer?

   Toad realizes the car he has flagged down is the very one he had stolen from the Red Lion that

   landed him in jail.

10. As Toad is flung through the air from the crash, what animal does he think he might become? What does he do as soon as he lands? What is his reaction when he stops to think about having wrecked the car?

    As Toad sails through the air, he likes the motion and wonders if he will turn into a Toad-bird.

    After landing, "He picked himself up rapidly and set off running across country as hard as he

    could." When Toad stops to think about what he has done, "he began to giggle, and from

    giggling he took to laughing, and he laughed till he had to sit down under a hedge." He was

    full of self-admiration for tricking the men into letting him drive.

11. When Toad flees, he runs right into the river. Where does he pull himself out of the river? Who is there?

    Toad pulls himself out of the river at a big dark hole in the bank. In the hole, he finds Water Rat.

SOCRATIC DISCUSSION QUESTIONS (LOGIC | Dialectic)

1. Explain two lessons and their consequences Grahame is teaching through Toad's interactions with the barge-woman.

   One lesson Grahame teaches is the danger of lying. When Toad lies and says he is a

   washerwoman and boasts about how much he loves it and is good at it, the consequence is

   the barge-woman has Toad do her wash. Another lesson Grahame teaches is not to lose your

   temper and be cheeky. When the barge-woman mocks Toad for his poor washing, Toad loses

   self-control, calls her fat, and reveals his identity. The consequence is that the barge-woman

   tosses him in the river. (Other lessons are possible, such as pride or self-control.)

2. The Bible has much to say about our tongues. Read Proverbs 21:23, Proverbs 15:1, and Matthew 15:11. How do these passages relate to Toad's character? Use examples from the chapter to support your answer.

Proverbs 21:23 says that he who guards his tongue keeps himself out of trouble. In Chapter

10, Toad lies to the barge-woman, which leads him to the trouble of having to do her laundry.

Proverbs 15:1 says a soft answer will turn away wrath, but harsh words stir up anger. When the

barge-woman laughs at Toad's struggle to do her laundry, "Toad's temper, which had been

simmering viciously for some time, now fairly boiled over, and he lost all control of himself."

He calls her fat and reveals the truth about who he is, a toad, and is tossed into the river as

a result. Matthew 15:11 says the words that come out of the mouth defile a person. When

Toad lies to the gentlemen who own the motor-car and asks if he can drive, he defiles himself

because he knows that this will lead to sin. Toad knows he has no self-control behind the

wheel, yet he asks to drive anyway.

3. Do you think, after being chased by the chauffeur and the humiliation of falling in the river, that Toad will finally show growth in character? Why or why not?

Answers will vary.

4. Extra Credit: Write another stanza continuing Toad's conceited poem. Make sure you follow the same rhyme scheme Toad uses.

Answers will vary.

Chapter 11

READING NOTES

1. **stoat** – the most common type of mustelid; very thin, about half the size of a rabbit; chestnut-brown coat that turns white in the winter; fierce fighter, killing prey with a sharp bite behind the ear; will attack much larger prey

2. **weasel** – the smallest of the three mustelids; thin, muscular body; small head; reddish coat; will attack larger prey; kills most prey underground

3. **ferret** – the largest of the mustelids; about the length of a small cat; cream-colored coat, with black tips of fur; very good hearing and a strong sense of smell; hunts mainly at night; very good climber; kills small mammals

WORDS TO BE DEFINED

Definitions Bank

a low wall or railing along an edge	easily angered
an accessory item of equipment or dress	food
calmed; made to feel better	in a degrading way; shamefully
carelessly or jauntily	overdone
deceptive strategies for the purpose of escaping or evading	repentance; sorrow over one's sins

---

1. such escapes, such disguises, such **subterfuges**

   deceptive strategies for the purpose of escaping or evading

2. the rusty black bonnet perched **rakishly** over one eye

   carelessly or jauntily

3. **ignominiously** flung into the water

   in a degrading way; shamefully

4. two stoats leaning over the **parapet** of the bridge

   a low wall or railing along an edge

5. said the good-natured Rat, already **appeased**

   calmed; made to feel better

6. at this very serious and **portentous** style of greeting

   overdone

7. he's wanting his **victuals**

   food
   _____

8. shaken by sobs of **contrition**

   repentance; sorrow over one's sins
   _____

9. He's a good boy, but very light and **volatile**

   easily angered
   _____

10. with every fresh **accoutrement** he produced

    an accessory item of equipment or dress
    _____

📖 *Read Chapter 11, marking the text in key places according to the method taught in "How to Mark a Book."*

COMPREHENSION QUESTIONS

1. As soon as Rat pulls Toad to safety, what does Toad begin to do?

   Toad begins to tell of his troubles since he had last seen his friends. He tells of the cleverness

   and courage he showed in outwitting everyone.
   _____

2. After Toad cleans himself up, what does he think as he examines himself in the looking-glass? What does this show about his character growth?

   Gazing into the looking-glass, Toad contemplates "himself with pride and pleasure, and

   thinking what utter idiots all the people must have been to have ever mistaken him for one

   moment for a washerwoman." Once again, Toad lacks character growth.
   _____

3. What surprising news does Rat have for Toad?

   Rat informs Toad that the Wild Wooders have taken over Toad Hall.
   _____

4. As Toad begins to tear up when he learns what is happening at Toad Hall, what onomatopoeia does Grahame use?

   The onomatopoeia Grahame uses for Toad's tears is "plop! plop!"
   _____

5. Who are the Wild Wooders? How does the Wild Wooders' opinion of Toad differ from the River-bankers' opinion of Toad?

     The Wild Wooders are the stoats, weasels, and ferrets. The Wild Wooders believe Toad got

     what he deserved and that he will never get out of prison. The River-bankers think Toad was

     treated unjustly.

6. How did Toad's loyal friends try to protect Toad Hall? What happened?

     Toad's friends moved into Toad Hall to take care of it in Toad's absence, but one dark night, "a

     band of weasels, armed to the teeth" with "a body of desperate ferrets" and "a company of

     skirmishing stoats" crept up, rushed in, beat Badger and Mole with sticks, and ran them off,

     taking over Toad Hall.

7. What is the hierarchy of the stoats, weasels, and ferrets at Toad Hall?

     At Toad Hall, the weasels seem to be in charge. The stoats and ferrets remain mostly outside

     Toad Hall, acting as sentries around the perimeter.

8. What surprising news does Badger have for Toad?

     Badger tells Toad of a secret underground entrance to Toad Hall.

9. Who does Badger send to spy on Toad Hall, and what does he find out?

     Badger sends Otter disguised as a chimney sweep to spy on the Wild Wooders at Toad Hall.

     Otter learns that there will soon be a big banquet for the Chief Weasel's birthday and that all

     the weasels will be gathered in the dining hall, unarmed and unsuspecting of any attack.

10. What does Mole use to disguise himself so that he can talk to the Wild Wooders at Toad Hall?

     Mole dresses himself in the old washerwoman clothes.

SOCRATIC DISCUSSION QUESTIONS (LOGIC | Dialectic)

1. Has there been any growth in Toad's character from Chapter 10 to Chapter 11? Support your answer with examples from the book.

   Toad's character has not shown any growth from Chapter 10 to Chapter 11. He is prideful and

   boastful when he tells Ratty of all his adventures. He embellishes his story when he tells Mole.

   He is jealous of Mole when he earns praise from Badger.

2. When Ratty begins to tell Toad about what has happened to Toad Hall since he has been gone, he says, "When you — got — into that — that — trouble of yours ... I mean, when you — disappeared from society for a time, over that misunderstanding about a — a machine, you know — " Why do you think Ratty has such a hard time saying the words *prison, criminal,* and *jail*? How might Ratty's inability to say the hard truth affect Toad's character? Compare this to a situation you've observed in life.

   Answers will vary. Ratty wants to show loyalty and support to his friend. He tries to downplay

   Toad's behavior and the consequences that he received. Ratty's inability to say what truly

   happened encourages Toad to not take responsibility for his actions. This could be compared

   to a parent who does not discipline a child, so the child's behavior continues to escalate

   because there are no boundaries.

3. Mole shows great growth in Chapter 11. What does Mole do to show himself to be the cleverest animal of all? Do you think his action is wise? How does Toad feel about the praise Mole receives?

   Mole shows growth when he dresses as the washerwoman and visits the stoats and ferrets. His

   action is wise because he creates fear and dissension in their ranks, making them believe there will

   be a huge attack on Toad Hall. When Badger praises Mole, Toad is "simply wild with jealousy."

Chapter 12

READING NOTES

1. **Ulysses** – Odysseus in Homer's *Iliad* and *Odyssey*, called Ulysses in Virgil's *Aeneid*

2. **cutlass** – a short, curved sword; machete

3. **truncheon** – a billy club

4. **cudgel** – a short, heavy club; Badger's weapon of choice

5. **trifle** – a dessert, usually consisting of cake soaked in wine or spirits, layered with custard and fruit

6. **cold tongue** – the cooked and cooled flesh of an ox or sheep's tongue, used as food

WORDS TO BE DEFINED

Definitions Bank	
a dressing room or bedroom	noisy
calmly	perfect
expression arising from deep emotion, especially intended to flatter	unjust defamation of character
	wild partying with drinking of liquor
low or dishonorable	

1. the Badger only remarked **placidly** _____ calmly _____

2. where their unconscious enemies were **carousing** _ wild partying with drinking of liquor ___

   _____

3. matchless valour, **consummate** strategy ____ perfect _____

4. hear the **tumultuous** applause _____ noisy _____

5. Mole is now sitting in the blue **boudoir** ____ a dressing room or bedroom _____

6. He sang this very loud, with great **unction** __ expression arising from deep emotion, especially

   intended to flatter _____

7. This was a **base** libel on Badger _____ low or dishonorable _____

8. This was a base **libel** on Badger _____unjust defamation of character_____

📖 *Read Chapter 12, marking the text in key places according to the method taught in "How to Mark a Book."*

COMPREHENSION QUESTIONS

1. What is Badger's weapon of choice?

    Badger chooses the cudgel or as he calls it, "this here stick."

2. What two mishaps does Toad have as the expedition starts?

    First, Toad falls into the river, making a great commotion; then he runs into the others in the

    secret passage, causing chaos and confusion, and almost gets shot by Badger.

3. Describe each of the Heroes, as they begin their attack on Toad Hall.

    Badger is armed with a cudgel, whiskers bristling. Rat is "desperate and determined, his

    belt bulging with weapons of every age and every variety." Mole rushes in, black and grim,

    brandishing his stick and shouting, "A Mole! A Mole!" Toad is swollen to twice his ordinary

    size, "emitting Toad-whoops" and shouting the words to the Chief Weasel's mocking song

    about him.

4. How does Mole distinguish himself as a leader again?

    The Mole shows himself to be a leader when he takes on the task of having the captured Wild

    Wooders put the bedrooms back to right and again when he takes on the task of rewriting the

    invitations that Toad had ruined.

5. Toad was going to object to writing invitations to the celebration. Why does he change his mind?

    Toad does not want the chore of writing the invitations until he realizes he can control the

    agenda of the party and all the speeches he can give about himself and his adventures.

6. After confronting Toad about the selfish invitations, Badger and Ratty firmly explain to Toad that the party is not about him and that it is time to turn over a new leaf. How do these boundaries affect Toad?

Toad understands that he is trapped and his friends see through him. He admits that he has

been conquered and says, "You are right, I know, and I am wrong. Henceforth I will be a very

different Toad. My friends, you shall never have occasion to blush for me again. But, O dear, O

dear, this is a hard world!"

7. How are those who helped Toad on his journey home from prison compensated?

The gaoler's daughter is sent a handsome gold chain and locket set with pearls and a letter

that is modest, grateful, and appreciative. The engine-driver is thanked and compensated.

Even the barge-woman is found and repaid for the stolen horse.

8. Give evidence that the four Heroes become a legend in the Wild Wood.

When the four friends stroll in the Wild Wood, they are respectfully greeted by its inhabitants,

and mother weasels point them out to their babies as "the great Mr. Toad! ... the gallant

Water Rat ... the famous Mr. Mole." Mothers also use Mr. Badger's name to frighten their

misbehaving children.

SOCRATIC DISCUSSION QUESTIONS (LOGIC | Dialectic)

1. Why do you think Grahame chose "The Return of Ulysses" as the title of Chapter 12? How does the title relate to the chapter?

"The Return of Ulysses" makes a humorous comparison between Toad's return to Toad Hall

and the return of Odysseus (Ulysses) to his home at the end of Homer's *Odyssey*. Like Ulysses,

Toad returns to his friends in disguise. Ulysses returns home as a beggar and Toad as the

washerwoman. Also like Ulysses, Toad arrives to a home filled with his enemies and enlists the

help of old friends to avenge himself and take back what is his.

2. How does the order in which the animals enter the passage reflect their standing in the group? What does the order suggest about Mole and Toad?

The animals enter with Badger in the lead, followed by Mole, then Rat, and finally Toad. This

order shows the level of importance in the group, with Badger being the most important and

giving the orders. Having Mole next demonstrates Mole's growth in character. Badger even

says, "Mole first, 'cos I'm very pleased with him." Mole has even passed Rat in importance.

Last is Toad, showing how his character has yet to have grown or changed at all. Badger even

threatens to send him back if he "chatter(s) so much as usual."

3. Read Proverbs 17:28 and Proverbs 10:19. How do these Scripture verses apply to Toad's behavior at the banquet hall? What do you think Toad has learned from the experience of holding his tongue?

The Scriptures teach that restraining your words is wise and that even a fool who keeps silent is

considered wise and intelligent. At the banquet, rather than boasting as he normally would, Toad

gives credit for the recapture of Toad Hall to Badger, Mole, and Rat. He shows humility by saying

that he "merely served in the ranks and did little or nothing." Toad realizes that by not bragging,

he gains the respect of Badger and Rat "and this gave him the greatest satisfaction."

4. What lesson about humility does Grahame convey through Toad's character in Chapter 12?

Though Toad hopes to elevate himself by telling grand stories and always boasting and

bragging about his adventures and his escapes, Grahame uses Toad in Chapter 12 to teach that

being humble and giving others credit is what truly earns respect.

RHETORIC | Expression

The student expresses in his or her own words the Central One Idea with supporting details.

❶ CENTRAL ONE IDEA

1. In a paragraph, **summarize** Chapters 10-12.

    Answers will vary. Here is an example:

    Chapter 10 begins with Toad waking up in the woods, still lost and trying to find his way home.

    His attempts at finding a ride are all ruined by his pride, and he ends up in the river, where

    he reunites with his friend Rat. Rat tells Toad the sad predicament of Toad Hall in Chapter

    11. Stoats and weasels have taken over his home, but Badger soon tells Toad of the plans to

    reclaim Toad Hall. Chapter 11 ends with Rat, Toad, Badger, and Mole preparing to take back

    Toad's home. Their victory is confirmed in Chapter 12, when the four animals bravely ambush

    the stoats and weasels and kick them out. After they spruce up Toad Hall to its former state,

    Badger plans a banquet to celebrate. Toad becomes a quieter, more respectable animal, and

    the story of the friends' valiant efforts is told to all young animals in the years after.

2. Write the **Central One Idea** of Chapters 10-12 in a complete sentence.

    Answers will vary.

3. List three or four points that support your determination of the Central One Idea.

    Answers will vary. Support for the Teacher's Central One Idea: (1) Ratty explains that Toad's

    actions are becoming an embarrassment to the friends, but that his friends never stopped

    believing he would find a way to return home. (2) Though Toad boasts and brags about his

    adventures, Mole still listens like a good friend. (3) Toad is jealous of the praise that Badger

    is heaping on Mole, but Toad puts his selfish feelings aside and thanks his friend for his

    cleverness. (4) Toad creates invitations for the victory party that makes himself the star of the

    evening. Despite this selfish act, Mole spends his afternoon rewriting the invitations.

❶ CENTRAL ONE IDEA (as expressed by the teacher)

Despite personal faults and flaws, friends give grace and stick by each other no matter what.

_____

_____

ESSAY OPTION

1. **Independent Essay:** When Toad enters the party at the end of the novel, he has resolved that he will not boast or sing songs about himself, but instead praise his friends. As the party continues, Toad finally earns the respect from Badger he so desired. Look up Proverbs 17:28 and 10:19. Write an essay explaining how these Scriptures reflect the change in Toad's character by the end of _The Wind in the Willows_.

Student Essay:
(A good essay length is between 2-3 pages.)

Answers will vary.

_____

_____

_____

_____

_____

_____

_____

_____

_____

_____

_____

_____

_____

_____

MEMORIZATION & RECITATION

David M. Wright

INSTRUCTIONS

Select a passage (or 2-3 small passages from different places) from *The Wind in the Willows* that you particularly like or feel some connection to. Follow the steps below to memorize the passage(s). The lined page following this is for you to *practice* writing the passage(s) to help you memorize it, as the steps below explain. Page 95 is for your *final handwritten version* of the passage(s), written with your best penmanship after you have memorized the entire passage(s).

You have three choices regarding the number of lines and the letter grade:

A: 17-20 lines   B: 12-16 lines   C: 9-11 lines

HOW TO MEMORIZE A PASSAGE

1. **Read the passage several times in order to understand the main idea.**
   - It is much easier to memorize something you understand!
   - Read the passage both silently and aloud.

2. **Get to know the rhythm, tone, and general structure of the passage.**
   - Knowing the rhythm and sound of the passage will greatly increase your ability to remember it.

3. a. **Read the first sentence several times until you memorize it.** (both silently and aloud)

   b. **Read the second sentence a number of times until you memorize it.** (both silently and aloud)

   c. **Recite the two sentences together.** (both silently and aloud)

   d. **Repeat steps a-c for the next two sentences.**

   e. **Write the four sentences down with good penmanship.**

4. **Repeat steps a-e for each set of four sentences.**

5. **After memorizing each set of four sentences, recite the previous four sentences and the new four sentences together.** (both silently and aloud)

6. **Continue until the entire passage is memorized.**

7. **Have your parent, sibling, or friend sit down and listen to you recite your passage!**

8. **Be sure to ask your teacher to set aside a class session for everyone to recite his or her passage!**

PRACTICE SPACE FOR WRITING THE PASSAGE

Final Memorized Passage

Use Your Best Penmanship!

QUIZZES &
TESTS

(Reproducible)

QUIZ: Grahame Biography & Literary Terms

Name:_____ Date: _____ Score: _____

TRUE OR FALSE (1 pt. each)

_____ 1. Kenneth Grahame was born in Edinburgh, Scotland, on March 8, 1859.

_____ 2. Because of his mother's death and his father turning to alcohol, Grahame and his siblings went to live with their grandmother.

_____ 3. His time living with his grandmother was spent in a small London apartment where Grahame felt his only escape from the city noise was going to the library.

_____ 4. Because he could not afford college, Grahame took a job at a bank, where he was very successful.

_____ 5. Grahame's most successful short story was "The Reluctant Dragon."

_____ 6. Grahame's only son was born deaf in one ear.

_____ 7. Before writing the book, Grahame told bedtime stories to his son about Mole, Rat, and Toad.

_____ 8. Many scholars believe the lessons in *The Wind in the Willows* were meant to teach Grahame's son about the world, maturity, and respectability.

_____ 9. U.S. President William Howard Taft endorsed *The Wind in the Willows*, helping the book to become a success.

_____ 10. Grahame's son died just before his fifteenth birthday.

_____ 11. Grahame dealt with his grief by writing several more short stories about Toad.

_____ 12. Grahame died on July 6, 1932, and was buried beside his son's grave.

FILL IN THE BLANK (1 pt. each)

Word Bank		
alliteration	foreshadowing	plot
allusion	imagery	setting
anthropomorphized	metaphor	simile
characters	onomatopoeia	
epiphany	personification	

Choose the correct term for each definition.

_____ 1. a moment of insight, discovery, or revelation

_____ 2. a reference to any person, place, or thing (literary, historical, or actual)

_____ 3. the comparison of two unlike things with the use of *like, as,* or *than*; shows that something unknown can be understood because it is similar to something known

_____ 4. the time and place of a literary work

_____ 5. a series of actions or related events that move the story forward

_____ 6. the use of indicative words or phrases that hint at something that will happen in the story; it sets the stage for the event without revealing the story or spoiling the suspense

_____ 7. a word or series of words referring to any sensory experience; direct or literal re-creation of physical experience

_____ 8. those taking part in the story

Choose the correct literary element for each example.

_____ 9. "plates on the dresser *grinned* at pots on the shelf"

_____ 10. "*Toad's rich,* we all know; but he's not a millionaire. And *he's a hopelessly bad driver,* and quite regardless of law and order."

_____ 11. "he had fallen in love at first sight with the *canary-colored cart*"

_____ 12. "The '*poop-poop*' rang with a brazen shout in their ears"

_____ 13. "The reserved rustic road was presently joined by a shy little brother in the shape of a canal, which took its hand and ambled along by its side in perfect confidence"

QUIZ: Chapters 1-2

Name:_____ Date: _____ Score: _____

VOCABULARY: Choose the correct definition for the underlined word. (1 pt. each)

1. "This was an <u>impromptu</u> affair"
   a. mocking
   b. careful
   c. crazy
   d. unplanned

2. "the <u>emancipated</u> Mole"
   a. liberated; freed
   b. respectful
   c. small
   d. spoiled

3. "<u>squandered</u> in trivialities"
   a. loved
   b. wasted
   c. annoyed
   d. wrecked

4. "that heavenly vision that has been <u>vouchsafed</u> me"
   a. granted
   b. excited
   c. encoded
   d. stolen

5. "Naturally a <u>voluble</u> animal"
   a. stuffed
   b. proud
   c. hopeless
   d. talkative

6. "he rambled busily ... across the <u>copses</u>"
   a. small groupings of trees
   b. dead bodies
   c. small, secluded valleys
   d. police officers

7. "the silvery shoulder and foamy tumble of a <u>weir</u>"
   a. a wolf-man
   b. a ditch running alongside a road
   c. a dam in a river
   d. a row of corn

8. "Nothing would please him but to <u>punt</u> all day and every day"
   a. to propel one's boat by using a pole against the river bottom
   b. a swimming stroke involving pushing against the river bottom with one's feet
   c. a type of motorboat used in swampy areas
   d. to row a boat backwards

9. "the hedgerows, the rolling <u>downs</u>!"
   a. certain types of oar strokes used with river boats
   b. rolling, grassy land
   c. cloudy, stormy days
   d. lands in a river bottom

10. "the dusty highway, the heath, the <u>common</u>"
    a. a road running through the center of a community
    b. a very plain type of house
    c. land owned or used by all the people of a community
    d. a certain language used by all members of a particular society

MULTIPLE CHOICE (1 pt. each)

1. What season is it when the book opens?
   a. winter
   b. spring
   c. summer
   d. fall

2. Which character takes on the role of a mentor?
   a. Ratty
   b. Mole
   c. Otter
   d. Toad

3. Which of the following is NOT one of the four worlds discussed in Chapter 1?
   a. River
   b. Wild Wood
   c. Village
   d. Wide World

4. Who says, "Believe me, my young friend, there is *nothing*—absolutely nothing—half so much worth doing as simply messing about in boats. Simply messing"?
   a. Ratty
   b. Mole
   c. Otter
   d. Toad

5. What is it that Rat does not want Mole to ever refer to again?
   a. Mole's underground home
   b. weasels, stoats, and foxes
   c. animal etiquette
   d. Wide World

6. At the opening of Chapter 2, what favor does Mole ask of Ratty?
   a. to teach him how to write poetry
   b. to take him to meet Toad
   c. to take him to meet Badger
   d. to buy him a canary-colored cart

7. What season is the opening of Chapter 2?
   a. winter
   b. spring
   c. summer
   d. fall

8. What does Toad request of Mole and Ratty?
   a. to travel on the open road with him
   b. to help him repair the paddock at Toad Hall
   c. to ride in a motor-car with him
   d. to punt on the river

9. What literary device is used in "he proceeded to play upon the inexperienced Mole as on a harp"?
   a. allusion
   b. alliteration
   c. simile
   d. foreshadowing

10. What caused Toad's great epiphany?
   a. the canary-colored cart
   b. the rapturous simplicity of the primitive life
   c. the motor-car
   d. traveling by train

SHORT ANSWER

1. In a complete sentence, describe Toad's character. (2 pts.)

    _____

    _____

    _____

    _____

    _____

    _____

2. In complete sentences, explain how Toad's view of the open road changes. (3 pts.)

    _____

    _____

    _____

    _____

    _____

    _____

QUIZ: Chapters 3-4

Name:_____ Date: _____ Score: _____

VOCABULARY: Choose the correct definition for the underlined word. (1 pt. each)

1. "the <u>languorous</u> siesta of hot midday"
   a. noisy
   b. disturbing
   c. long; dull
   d. weary; weak

2. "the <u>verdant</u> banks of dream-rivers"
   a. rusty
   b. copper
   c. green
   d. muddy

3. "'Really Rat,' said the Mole quite <u>pettishly</u>."
   a. cruelly
   b. giddily
   c. mockingly
   d. in a bad-tempered way

4. "the astonished and ... <u>incredulous</u> Mole"
   a. unbelieving
   b. irresponsible
   c. mischievous
   d. overjoyed

5. "Rat attacked a snow-bank ... with <u>ardour</u>."
   a. weariness
   b. enthusiasm
   c. great frustration
   d. warm delight

6. "he had been busy laying a <u>repast</u>"
   a. lawn
   b. blanket
   c. meal
   d. campsite

7. "The Mole <u>assented</u> heartily"
   a. disagreed
   b. ate vigorously
   c. agreed
   d. complained

8. "the whole mass of the Wild Wood, dense, <u>menacing</u>, compact"
   a. simple in design
   b. threatening
   c. disjointed
   d. expansive

9. "more to <u>oblige</u> the Rat than for any other reason"
   a. to be kindly accommodating
   b. to confuse by teasing
   c. to comfort because of sorrow
   d. to signal a warning

10. "I had to <u>cuff</u> his head once or twice"
    a. to strike with an open hand
    b. to pet with gentle affection
    c. to translate
    d. to fill in missing information

MULTIPLE CHOICE (1 pt. each)

1. What quality does Badger show when listening to Rat and Mole tell their story of how they got stuck in the woods?
   a. nervousness
   b. weariness
   c. wisdom
   d. impatience

2. After his experience in the Wild Wood, where does Mole learn that he belongs?
   a. in safe, domesticated places
   b. in a riverboat (Ratty was right all along!)
   c. at Toad Hall
   d. in wild, unknown lands

3. What does Mole like most about winter?
   a. hot apple cider
   b. the sound of the winter wind
   c. all the land uncovered and bare
   d. the beautiful snowfall

4. How is Mole best described?
   a. rude
   b. wise
   c. brave
   d. childlike

5. Who said, "Any friend of *mine* walks where he likes in this country, or I'll know the reason why"?
   a. Ratty
   b. Mole
   c. Badger
   d. Toad

6. About whom was Rat speaking when he said, "The best of fellows! But you must not only take him *as* you find him, but *when* you find him"?
   a. Toad
   b. Rabbit
   c. Otter
   d. Badger

7. About whom were the friends speaking when they said, "Smashes, or machines? ... O, well, after all, it's the same thing — with _____"?
   a. Badger
   b. Toad
   c. Otter
   d. Ratty

8. "Such a rich chapter it [the summer] had been" is an example of
   a. alliteration
   b. metaphor
   c. onomatopoeia
   d. simile

9. "Purple loosestrife arrived early, shaking luxuriant tangled locks" is an example of
   a. simile
   b. metaphor
   c. onomatopoeia
   d. personification

10. "diffident and delaying dog-rose stepped delicately" is an example of
    a. alliteration
    b. metaphor
    c. onomatopoeia
    d. personification

SHORT ANSWER

1. List the three clues Ratty uses to determine they are at Badger's door? (3 pts.)

    _____

    _____

    _____

    _____

    _____

2. In a complete sentence, explain the common bond between Mole and Badger. (2 pts.)

    _____

    _____

    _____

    _____

QUIZ: Chapters 5-6

Name:_____ Date: _____ Score: _____

VOCABULARY: Choose the correct definition for the underlined word. (1 pt. each)

1. "Close against the white blind hung a bird-cage, clearly silhouetted, every wire, perch, and <u>appurtenance</u> distinct and recognizable"
   a. accessory
   b. shadow
   c. curtain
   d. bar

2. "by a flow of cheerful talk and <u>anecdote</u> endeavoured to beguile his spirits back and make the weary way seem shorter"
   a. lavish attention
   b. a short humorous or interesting story
   c. a tall tale
   d. deep disdain

3. "The Badger's <u>caustic</u>, not to say brutal, remarks may be imagined, and therefore passed over"
   a. kind and compassionate
   b. lighthearted and witty
   c. sarcastic
   d. overly parental

4. Toad was accused of "gross <u>impertinence</u> to the rural police."
   a. outlandish trickery
   b. insulting, irreverent conduct
   c. improper physical appearance
   d. the act of fleeing arrest

5. "Poor Mole stood alone in the road, his heart torn <u>asunder</u>"
   a. deeply regretful
   b. discouraged; hopeless
   c. torn in two
   d. sorrowful; mournful

6. "No bread!" groaned the Mole <u>dolorously</u>
   a. hungry; famished
   b. sorrowfully; mournfully
   c. shamefully
   d. enthusiastically

7. "astonished and dismayed at the violence of Mole's <u>paroxysm</u> of grief"
   a. shame
   b. worriedness
   c. stoic response
   d. sudden outburst

8. "His hearty accents <u>faltered</u> and fell away"
   a. wavered; weakened
   b. strengthened
   c. came to a sudden end
   d. accused

9. "He did it awfully well," said the <u>crestfallen</u> Rat.
   a. proud
   b. ashamed
   c. determined; unrelenting
   d. heartfelt

10. "whom we see <u>cowering</u> in the dock before us"
   a. showing pride
   b. wincing as in pain
   c. crying uncontrollably
   d. crouching or shrinking away in fear

MULTIPLE CHOICE (1 pt. each)

1. What does the court say was Toad's worst offense?
   a. running away from home
   b. cheeking the police
   c. failing to pay his bill at the restaurant
   d. stealing the motor-car

2. What difficult choice does Mole have to make in Chapter 5: Dulce Domum?
   a. to move back home or to continue staying on the river
   b. to trust Ratty or to find his own way home
   c. to go find his home or to go on with Ratty
   d. to go through the village or to go through the fields

3. What do Toad's friends do when they realize he refuses to change his ways?
   a. They give up and leave him to his own foolishness.
   b. They remove him from Toad Hall.
   c. They imprison him in his room.
   d. They take him to a doctor.

4. What literary device is used here: "even the delicate tips of his plumped-out plumage pencilled plainly on the illuminated screen"?
   a. metaphor
   b. alliteration
   c. rhyme
   d. onomatopoeia

5. Where is Toad when he sees the fated motor-car that causes him such trouble?
   a. riding on a barge
   b. Red Lion
   c. on the river
   d. riding on a train

6. Which of the following is NOT a way that Ratty proves his friendship to Mole in Chapter 5: Dulce Domum?
   a. He tells Mole a bedtime story to help him sleep.
   b. He helps Mole clean and straighten his home.
   c. He backtracks in the cold to help Mole find his underground home.
   d. He sends out a field-mouse to buy food and drink for Mole's guests.

7. What does Ratty say when he realizes he has caused Mole's distress?

    a. "What a child you are being!"

    b. "What a *pig* I have been!"

    c. "I am sorry, old chap. Do forgive me and let's get to the river now!"

    d. "What on earth is causing such a commotion?"

8. What literary technique is used in the following passage: "'[Toad will] be so conceited … that he may commit any folly.' … So spoke the Badger, not knowing what the future held in store"?

    a. foreshadowing

    b. onomatopoeia

    c. personification

    d. metaphor

9. Which of the following is Toad called in court?

    a. a confounded coward

    b. the vilest of villains

    c. an ignorant fool

    d. an incorrigible rogue

10. What does the title *Dulce Domum* mean in Latin?

    a. Sweet Dome

    b. A Heart for Home

    c. Home Is Where the Heart Is

    d. Sweet Home

SHORT ANSWER

1. In complete sentences, explain three ways that Ratty shows his friendship to Mole in Chapter 5: Dulce Domum. (3 pts.)

_____

_____

_____

_____

_____

2. In Chapter 6, Toad is held accountable for his actions in a courtroom. While Toad receives time for stealing the car and endangering the public, his worst crime was "cheeking" the police. In complete sentences, explain the message Grahame was sending to his son through Toad's experience and consequences? (2 pts.)

_____

_____

_____

_____

QUIZ: Chapters 7-8

Name:_____ Date: _____ Score: _____

VOCABULARY: Choose the correct definition for the underlined word. (1 pt. each)

1. "till sunshine should fall on them at last and send them off to their well-earned <u>repose</u>"
   a. joy
   b. wages; payment
   c. rest
   d. meal

2. "some <u>august</u> Presence was very, very near"
   a. summerlike
   b. deserving of reverence
   c. ancient
   d. terrifying

3. "Toad found himself <u>immured</u> in a dank … dungeon"
   a. frozen
   b. hidden
   c. desperately lost
   d. enclosed

4. "with its [the breeze's] soft touch came instant <u>oblivion</u>"
   a. happiness
   b. total forgetfulness
   c. intense heat
   d. peaceful warmth

5. "in such an <u>audacious</u> manner"
   a. shy; timid
   b. rude or uncouth
   c. recklessly bold
   d. eager

6. "The chaff and the humorous <u>sallies</u> to which he was subjected"
   a. witty remarks
   b. long outings
   c. older sisters
   d. insults

7. "a <u>capricious</u> little breeze, dancing up from the surface of the water"
   a. steadfast
   b. constantly changing; unpredictable
   c. blustery
   d. cool and refreshing

8. "the only <u>stipulation</u> the old lady made being that she should be gagged"
   a. mix-up
   b. deviation
   c. joking
   d. condition in an agreement

9. "Toad was very much the same <u>sanguine</u>, self-satisfied animal"
   a. lazy
   b. picky
   c. outgoing
   d. melancholy

10. "a <u>jaunt</u> on the river"
   a. long journey; quest
   b. fishing expedition
   c. a holy journey
   d. short pleasure journey; outing

MULTIPLE CHOICE (1 pt. each)

1. When Chapter 7 begins, it is past ten at night and Mole is lying on the river bank when Ratty appears. From where had the Water Rat just come?
   a. a full day of boating on the river
   b. writing poetry
   c. dinner at Otter's house
   d. Wild Wood

2. Why are Ratty and Mole concerned about Little Portly?
   a. Otter has searched everywhere and has seen no signs of him.
   b. Portly is not a very good swimmer.
   c. There are traps.
   d. all of the above

3. What do Ratty and Mole do when they see the piper?
   a. They worship him.
   b. They ask him as many questions as they can about life.
   c. They call their friends to come see.
   d. They run and hide.

4. How does Toad escape the policemen who are chasing the train?
   a. He hides underneath the engine while it's moving.
   b. He jumps off into the woods.
   c. He pushes the engine-driver off and takes over.
   d. He hides in the coal piles.

5. How does Toad escape the dungeon?
   a. Ratty and Mole pay the judge to sign his release.
   b. He tunnels his way out through the floor.
   c. He knocks out the jailer and climbs out through the vents.
   d. He disguises himself as a washerwoman and walks out.

6. How does the piper ensure that the animals will still be happy after losing sight of him?
   a. He gives Ratty his pipes to keep.
   b. He gives them an autographed photo of himself.
   c. He makes them forget ever having seen him.
   d. He comes home to stay with them on the river.

7. Why does the gaoler's daughter want to help Toad?
   a. She falls in love with Toad and wants to marry him.
   b. She hates the prison warden and wants to cause problems.
   c. She's fond of animals and wants to teach him pet tricks.
   d. She thinks Toad is a famous war hero.

8. Who is the piper, and what is his relationship to the animals in the story?
   a. A farmer; he wants to take them as pets.
   b. Mr. Tumnus; he's a spying fawn.
   c. Pan; he's their god.
   d. The Pied Piper of Hamlin; he plans to lead them into the river.

9. What does the gaoler's daughter say is Toad's chief fault?

   a. He can't swim.

   b. He dreams too much.

   c. He's never happy.

   d. He talks too much.

10. How does Toad react when he first realizes he is in a dungeon?

    a. He throws a temper tantrum and refuses to eat.

    b. He swears to own the prison one day.

    c. He violently attacks the prison guard.

    d. He makes friends with his fellow prisoners.

SHORT ANSWER

1. Explain why Pan wipes the memories of the animals he helps. (2 pts.)

_____

_____

_____

_____

2. In Chapter 8, the gaoler's daughter takes pity on Toad and brings him a tray of tea and toast. Grahame writes, "The smell of that buttered toast simply talked to Toad, and with no uncertain voice; talked of warm kitchens, of breakfasts on bright frosty mornings, of cosy parlor firesides on winter evenings." Using complete sentences, explain the literary device(s) Grahame uses in this passage. (3 pts.)

_____

_____

_____

_____

_____

_____

_____

_____

QUIZ: Chapter 9

Name:_____ Date: _____ Score: _____

VOCABULARY: Choose the correct definition for the underlined word. (1 pt. each)

1. "The beat and quiver of impatient <u>pinions</u>"
   a. wings or feathers
   b. fingers
   c. a type of English leather shoes
   d. fleeting thoughts

2. "suggested the Water Rat <u>wistfully</u>"
   a. hopeless
   b. with sadness
   c. at ease
   d. worrisome

3. "now ere the <u>irrevocable</u> moment passes"
   a. reversible
   b. holy
   c. unable to be taken back
   d. temporary

4. "an <u>epitome</u> of my highly-colored life"
   a. ideal example
   b. opposite of
   c. distraction
   d. previous

5. "a <u>blithe some</u> step forward"
   a. mournful
   b. blundering
   c. hasty
   d. happy and lighthearted

MULTIPLE CHOICE (1 pt. each)

1. The title of Chapter 9 is "Wayfarers All." Who are the wayfarers?
   a. The animals boating on the river.
   b. The animals preparing to hibernate.
   c. The animals the rabbits charge to pass the road.
   d. The animals preparing to migrate to the south.

2. Why is the Water Rat feeling restless?
   a. There is a feeling of change in the air.
   b. He has writer's block and is struggling to write a new poem.
   c. The lack of rain has kept the river too low to go boating.
   d. There are too many animals at the river bank at this time of year.

3. "Nature's Grand Hotel has its Season" is an example of
   a. simile
   b. personification
   c. metaphor
   d. onomatopoeia

4. Which of the following does NOT cause Ratty to be "possessed" for a time by the Sea Rat's tales?
   a. the lights reflected in the Sea Rat's eyes
   b. the colored light of the red wine in the Sea Rat's glass
   c. the sea-foam grey-green of the Sea Rat's eyes
   d. the music of the Sea Rat's sailing song

5. When speaking about the farm and river life, what does the Sea Rat mean when he says, "It is a goodly life that you lead, friend; no doubt the best in the world, if only you are strong enough to lead it!"
   a. that farming is honorable but difficult and requires great strength
   b. that living tied to one place all the time takes strength
   c. that the river's ebb and flow require strength to manage
   d. that dealing with all the migration of animals coming and going takes strength

6. How is Ratty different in Chapter 9 compared to Chapter 1?
   a. He longs to see the Wide World now.
   b. He hates the river.
   c. He has grown tired of poetry.
   d. He begins to crave fortune and fame.

7. How does Mole prove to be a true friend to Ratty at the end of Chapter 9?
   a. He encourages Ratty to go to sea even though he will miss him.
   b. He calls Badger to help him run off the Sea Rat.
   c. He prays to Pan for Ratty to have a safe journey.
   d. He treats Ratty similarly to how they treated Toad, dragging him inside the house until he comes to his senses.

8. What does Mole do to help Ratty?
   a. He has Badger guard the door so he cannot leave.
   b. Mole gives him paper and encourages Ratty to write poetry.
   c. He gives Ratty a compass for his travels.
   d. He has the field-mice go to town and get Ratty's favorite treats.

SHORT ANSWER

1. In what season does this chapter take place, and how does this reflect Ratty's season of life? (5 pts.)

    _____

    _____

    _____

    _____

    _____

    _____

2. When the swallows describe the pull of nature to the wonderful place in the south that they will be heading to, Ratty asks, "Why do you ever come back, then, at all?" What reason do the swallows give for their return? (2 pts.)

    _____

    _____

    _____

    _____

    _____

    _____

QUIZ: Chapters 10-11

Name:_____ Date: _____ Score: _____

VOCABULARY: Choose the correct definition for the underlined word. (1 pt. each)

1. "he was determined to be <u>prudent</u>"
   a. smart-witted; good at making fun of others
   b. avoiding detection at any cost
   c. sly; sneaky
   d. careful; wise

2. "I simply <u>dote</u> on it [doing laundry]."
   a. to doubt or disbelieve
   b. to despise or fear
   c. to write upon
   d. to be overly affectionate toward

3. "its chill was not sufficient to <u>quell</u> his proud spirit"
   a. to quiet or calm
   b. to decrease
   c. to exaggerate
   d. to fill with pleasure

4. "the barge-woman was <u>gesticulating</u> wildly"
   a. stomping in quick rhythm
   b. making crude jokes; mocking
   c. making gestures with arms and hands
   d. a series of loud shouts

5. "<u>ignominiously</u> flung into the water"
   a. in a degrading way; shamefully
   b. absentmindedly
   c. with great pleasure
   d. to handle gently as with something that is fragile

6. "He's a good boy, but very light and <u>volatile</u> in character"
   a. shy
   b. easily angered
   c. not clever
   d. overly verbal

7. "such escapes, such disguises, such <u>subterfuges</u>"
   a. deceptive strategies for the purpose of escaping or evading
   b. daring efforts
   c. rough terrain
   d. difficult circumstances

8. "said the good-natured Rat, already <u>appeased</u>"
   a. showing signs of agitation
   b. nodding off to sleep
   c. calmed; made to feel better
   d. ready to defend

9. "with every fresh <u>accoutrement</u> he produced"
   a. idea
   b. verbal insult
   c. accessory item of equipment or dress
   d. confession of faith

10. "shaken by sobs of <u>contrition</u>"
    a. repentance; sorrow over one's sins
    b. anger or rage
    c. embarrassment
    d. frustration

MULTIPLE CHOICE (1 pt. each)

1. At the opening of Chapter 10, where had Toad spent the night after escaping the train?
   a. in an abandoned motor-car
   b. in a hollow tree
   c. in a gipsy caravan
   d. on a barge

2. Why does Toad have to do the barge-woman's laundry?
   a. because he boasted that he loved to do laundry
   b. because he lost a bet
   c. in exchange for a ride on the barge
   d. because he wanted to help her

3. "They [the garments] smiled back at him out of the tub unconverted, happy in their original sin." This sentence contains an example of
   a. imagery
   b. alliteration
   c. personification
   d. metaphor

4. Toad sells the horse to the gipsy because he wants
   a. a ride to Toad Hall and a new cart
   b. money and a solid breakfast
   c. breakfast and a ride to Toad Hall
   d. money in his pockets and revenge on the barge-woman

5. Who does Toad meet at the end of Chapter 10 in the hole on the river?
   a. Otter
   b. Badger
   c. Mole
   d. Water Rat

6. What news does Rat have for Toad?
   a. Portly is missing.
   b. Toad Hall has been overrun with Wild Wooders.
   c. There was a fire at Toad Hall.
   d. The police are waiting for him at Toad Hall.

7. "And a large tear welled up in each of his eyes, overflowed and splashed on the table, plop! plop!" This is an example of
   a. epiphany
   b. onomatopoeia
   c. simile
   d. plot

8. Badger reveals that a secret passage leads from the river bank to where in Toad Hall?
   a. the butler's pantry
   b. the dining room
   c. the library
   d. the dungeon

9. What celebration does Otter learn will be taking place in Toad Hall?
   a. Chief Weasel's wedding
   b. Chief Weasel's daughter's wedding
   c. Chief Weasel's birthday
   d. Chief Stoat's birthday

SHORT ANSWER

1. When talking to the barge-woman, Toad says, "I simply dote on it. Never so happy as when I've got both arms in the wash-tub. But, then, it comes so easy to me! No trouble at all! A real pleasure, I assure you, ma'am!" How does this reveal the chief fault of Toad, according to the gaoler's daughter? (3 pts.)

_____

_____

_____

_____

_____

_____

2. Why does Badger regard Mole as clever and not foolish when Mole tells the stoats about an impending attack? (3 pts.)

_____

_____

_____

_____

_____

_____

FINAL EXAM

Name:_____ Date:_____ Score:_____

VOCABULARY: Choose the correct definition for the underlined word. (2 pts. each)

1. "This was an <u>impromptu</u> affair"
   a. mocking
   b. careful
   c. crazy
   d. unplanned

2. "Naturally a <u>voluble</u> animal"
   a. stuffed
   b. proud
   c. hopeless
   d. talkative

3. "the astonished and ... <u>incredulous</u> Mole"
   a. unbelieving
   b. irresponsible
   c. mischievous
   d. overjoyed

4. "more to <u>oblige</u> the Rat than for any other reason"
   a. to be kindly accommodating
   b. to confuse by teasing
   c. to comfort because of sorrow
   d. to signal a warning

5. "No bread!" groaned the Mole <u>dolorously</u>
   a. hungry; famished
   b. sorrowfully; mournfully
   c. shamefully
   d. enthusiastically

6. "The Badger's <u>caustic</u>, not to say brutal, remarks may be imagined, and therefore passed over"
   a. kind and compassionate
   b. lighthearted and witty
   c. painfully sarcastic
   d. overly parental

7. "some <u>august</u> Presence was very, very near"
   a. summerlike
   b. deserving of reverence
   c. ancient
   d. terrifying

8. "a <u>capricious</u> little breeze, dancing up from the surface of the water"
   a. steadfast
   b. constantly changing; unpredictable
   c. blustery
   d. cool and refreshing

9. "an <u>epitome</u> of my highly-colored life"
   a. ideal example
   b. opposite of
   c. distraction
   d. previous

10. "a <u>blithe some</u> step forward"
   a. mournful
   b. blundering
   c. hasty
   d. happy and lighthearted

11. "<u>ignominiously</u> flung into the water"
   a. in a degrading way; shamefully
   b. absentmindedly
   c. with great pleasure
   d. to handle gently as with something that is fragile

12. "its chill was not sufficient to <u>quell</u> his proud spirit"
   a. to quiet or calm
   b. to decrease
   c. to exaggerate
   d. to fill with pleasure

13. "the Badger only remarked <u>placidly</u>"
   a. coldly
   b. absentmindedly
   c. calmly
   d. sarcastically

14. A series of actions or related events that move the story forward:
   a. foreshadowing
   b. irony
   c. plot
   d. setting

15. A reference to any person, place, or thing (literary, historical, or actual):
   a. allusion
   b. personification
   c. epiphany
   d. metaphor

MULTIPLE CHOICE (2 pts. each)

1. How has Toad's character changed by the end of the story?
   a. He gave up his longing for adventure for good.
   b. He asked Badger to move into his home and help him stay out of trouble.
   c. He learned to stop boasting and be humble.
   d. He gave away his home and went to live on the river.
   e. He grew weary of his friends' interfering and turned against them.

2. According to Ratty, "There is *nothing*—absolutely nothing—half so much worth doing as simply ..." Complete the quote.
   a. lying under the stars.
   b. walking about with friends.
   c. sculling about on the river.
   d. messing about in boats.
   e. writing great poetry.

3. After whom in Kenneth Grahame's world is Toad's character patterned?

   a. Grahame himself
   b. Grahame's son
   c. Grahame's alcoholic father
   d. Grahame's boss at the bank
   e. Grahame's younger brother

4. At one point in the story, Ratty changes his opinion about something in a significant way. What is it?

   a. He goes from being disgusted with Toad's behavior to admiring Toad's brilliant escape.
   b. He goes from loving the river to fearing water for a brief moment.
   c. He goes from being disinterested in the Wide World to longing to go to sea and experience it.
   d. He goes from loving boats to preferring motor-cars.
   e. He goes from not trusting Badger to being Badger's good friend.

5. Which of the following is an example of personification in *The Wind in the Willows*?

   a. "plumped-out plumage pencilled plainly"
   b. "scene-pictures that succeeded each other"
   c. "while the river still chattered on to him, a babbling procession of the best stories in the world"
   d. "not knowing ... how much water ... was to run under bridges before Toad should sit at ease"
   e. "the pageant of the river bank"

6. Which of the following is a metaphor in *The Wind in the Willows*?

   a. "Such a rich chapter it [the summer] had been."
   b. "Their old haunts greeted them again ..."
   c. "the whole mass of the Wild Wood, dense, menacing, compact"
   d. "So spoke the Badger, not knowing what the future held in store ..."
   e. "the diffident and delaying dog-rose"

7. What was Toad's epiphany?

   a. his open road experience with the canary-colored cart
   b. his life-changing vision of the motor-car
   c. his grand moment taking back Toad Hall with his friends
   d. his courtroom experience
   e. his near-death experience when he falls into the river

8. At the end of Chapter 4: Mr. Badger, where has Mole learned that he belongs?

   a. adventuring in the Wide World
   b. on the river
   c. with his friends, wherever they may go
   d. in domesticated, civilized places of tilled field and hedgerow
   e. in the Wild Wood with Badger

9. Which of the following is NOT one of Toad's character flaws or faults?

   a. He is cruel to his friends.
   b. He talks too much.
   c. He is greedy and covetous.
   d. He is impulsive—acts without thinking first.
   e. He has no self-control.

10. Which of the following is an example of alliteration from *The Wind in the Willows*?

 a. "a hot sun seemed to be pulling everything ... up out of the earth towards him"

 b. "the diffident and delaying dog-rose"

 c. "it is impossible to say quite *all* you feel when your head is under water"

 d. "The ruddy brick floor smiled up at the smoky ceiling"

 e. "The pageant of the river bank had marched steadily along"

11. Which of the following is meant to describe Pan?

 a. "let each one of the crowd try and shout it very loud, in honor of an animal of whom you're justly proud"

 b. "Helper and healer, I cheer—Small waifs in the woodland wet"

 c. "like the very soul of Nature ... appearing to her children, a true Goddess"

 d. "Yellow feet a-quiver ... Busy in the river!"

 e. "draw us in by your fire to bide; Joy shall be yours in the morning"

12. Which of the following best describes Badger?

 a. cruel and violent; a bully of sorts

 b. silent, angry, and pouty most of the time

 c. serious, unchanging, stern but kind

 d. outgoing, but not a good listener

 e. greedy, always wanting a bigger home

13. Which of the following is NOT a character quality of Ratty?

 a. loves to be on the river

 b. poetic

 c. always a faithful friend

 d. observant

 e. loves to party

14. What clever thing does Mole do in Chapter 11?

 a. He disguises himself as a washerwoman and feeds false information to the stoats, ferrets, and weasels.

 b. He helps Toad get through the underground tunnel to safety.

 c. He sneaks into Toad Hall and spies on the weasels as they make party plans.

 d. He finds a back entrance into Toad Hall that isn't guarded.

 e. He sneaks up on the ferrets and single-handedly steals away with their weapons without getting caught.

15. Which of the following best describes the way Mole changes from the beginning of the story to the end?

 a. He grows to hate living underground.

 b. He quits being so selfish and boastful.

 c. He becomes a fun-loving party animal.

 d. He learns not to be so trusting of others.

 e. He "grows up" and becomes a brave leader.

SHORT ANSWER

1. Why does Mole prefer the Wild Wood in the winter over the summer? (5 pts.)

_____

_____

_____

2. The gaoler's daughter says that Toad's chief fault is that he talks too much. What is another fault Toad exhibits in the novel? Give an example to support your answer. (5 pts.)

_____

_____

_____

_____

_____

3. Proverbs 17:28 says, "Even a fool, when he holdeth his peace, is counted wise: and he that shutteth his lips is esteemed a man of understanding." At what event does Toad finally apply this wisdom? How do Badger and Ratty respond to this new Toad? (5 pts.)

_____

_____

_____

_____

ESSAY

1. In *The Wind in the Willows*, Grahame uses the four main characters to present a variety of life lessons and experiences. Choose a lesson that stood out to you. Give a brief summary of the events and characters involved. Explain both the lesson that Grahame is trying to convey and why you think this is an important lesson for a person to learn. (You may write in first person, as this is your opinion. There is not a right or wrong answer, only a supported or unsupported answer.) (15 pts.)

_____

_____

_____

_____

_____

_____

_____

_____

_____

_____

_____

_____

_____

_____

_____

_____

_____

_____

_____

_____

_____

_____

QUIZZES & TESTS KEY

QUIZ: Grahame Biography & Literary Terms — KEY

Name:_____ Date: _____ Score: _____

TRUE OR FALSE (1 pt. each)

____True____ **1.** Kenneth Grahame was born in Edinburgh, Scotland, on March 8, 1859.

____True____ **2.** Because of his mother's death and his father turning to alcohol, Grahame and his siblings went to live with their grandmother.

____False____ **3.** His time living with his grandmother was spent in a small London apartment where Grahame felt his only escape from the city noise was going to the library.

____True____ **4.** Because he could not afford college, Grahame took a job at a bank, where he was very successful.

____True____ **5.** Grahame's most successful short story was "The Reluctant Dragon."

____False____ **6.** Grahame's only son was born deaf in one ear.

____True____ **7.** Before writing the book, Grahame told bedtime stories to his son about Mole, Rat, and Toad.

____True____ **8.** Many scholars believe the lessons in *The Wind in the Willows* were meant to teach Grahame's son about the world, maturity, and respectability.

____False____ **9.** U.S. President William Howard Taft endorsed *The Wind in the Willows*, helping the book to become a success.

____False____ **10.** Grahame's son died just before his fifteenth birthday.

____False____ **11.** Grahame dealt with his grief by writing several more short stories about Toad.

____True____ **12.** Grahame died on July 6, 1932, and was buried beside his son's grave.

FILL IN THE BLANK (1 pt. each)

Word Bank		
alliteration	foreshadowing	plot
allusion	imagery	setting
anthropomorphized	metaphor	simile
characters	onomatopoeia	
epiphany	personification	

Choose the correct term for each definition.

_____epiphany_____	**1.**	a moment of insight, discovery, or revelation
_____allusion_____	**2.**	a reference to any person, place, or thing (literary, historical, or actual)
_____simile_____	**3.**	the comparison of two unlike things with the use of *like, as,* or *than*; shows that something unknown can be understood because it is similar to something known
_____setting_____	**4.**	the time and place of a literary work
_____plot_____	**5.**	a series of actions or related events that move the story forward
_____foreshadowing_____	**6.**	the use of indicative words or phrases that hint at something that will happen in the story; it sets the stage for the event without revealing the story or spoiling the suspense
_____imagery_____	**7.**	a word or series of words referring to any sensory experience; direct or literal re-creation of physical experience
_____characters_____	**8.**	those taking part in the story

Choose the correct literary element for each example.

_____personification_____	**9.**	"plates on the dresser *grinned* at pots on the shelf"
_____anthropomorphized_____	**10.**	"*Toad's rich,* we all know; but he's not a millionaire. And *he's a hopelessly bad driver,* and quite regardless of law and order."
_____alliteration_____	**11.**	"he had fallen in love at first sight with the *canary-colored cart*"
_____onomatopoeia_____	**12.**	"The '*poop-poop*' rang with a brazen shout in their ears"
_____metaphor_____	**13.**	"The reserved rustic road was presently joined by a shy little brother in the shape of a canal, which took its hand and ambled along by its side in perfect confidence"

QUIZ: Chapters 1-2 — KEY

Name:_____ Date: _____ Score: _____

VOCABULARY: Choose the correct definition for the underlined word. (1 pt. each)

1. "This was an <u>impromptu</u> affair"
   a. mocking
   b. careful
   c. crazy
   d. unplanned

2. "the <u>emancipated</u> Mole"
   a. liberated; freed
   b. respectful
   c. small
   d. spoiled

3. "<u>squandered</u> in trivialities"
   a. loved
   b. wasted
   c. annoyed
   d. wrecked

4. "that heavenly vision that has been <u>vouchsafed</u> me"
   a. granted
   b. excited
   c. encoded
   d. stolen

5. "Naturally a <u>voluble</u> animal"
   a. stuffed
   b. proud
   c. hopeless
   d. talkative

6. "he rambled busily ... across the <u>copses</u>"
   a. small groupings of trees
   b. dead bodies
   c. small, secluded valleys
   d. police officers

7. "the silvery shoulder and foamy tumble of a <u>weir</u>"
   a. a wolf-man
   b. a ditch running alongside a road
   c. a dam in a river
   d. a row of corn

8. "Nothing would please him but to <u>punt</u> all day and every day"
   a. to propel one's boat by using a pole against the river bottom
   b. a swimming stroke involving pushing against the river bottom with one's feet
   c. a type of motorboat used in swampy areas
   d. to row a boat backwards

9. "the hedgerows, the rolling <u>downs</u>!"
   a. certain types of oar strokes used with river boats
   b. rolling, grassy land
   c. cloudy, stormy days
   d. lands in a river bottom

10. "the dusty highway, the heath, the <u>common</u>"
    a. a road running through the center of a community
    b. a very plain type of house
    c. land owned or used by all the people of a community
    d. a certain language used by all members of a particular society

MULTIPLE CHOICE (1 pt. each)

1. What season is it when the book opens?
   a. winter
   b. spring
   c. summer
   d. fall

2. Which character takes on the role of a mentor?
   a. Ratty
   b. Mole
   c. Otter
   d. Toad

3. Which of the following is NOT one of the four worlds discussed in Chapter 1?
   a. River
   b. Wild Wood
   c. Village
   d. Wide World

4. Who says, "Believe me, my young friend, there is *nothing*—absolutely nothing—half so much worth doing as simply messing about in boats. Simply messing"?
   a. Ratty
   b. Mole
   c. Otter
   d. Toad

5. What is it that Rat does not want Mole to ever refer to again?
   a. Mole's underground home
   b. the weasels, stoats, and foxes
   c. animal etiquette
   d. Wide World

6. At the opening of Chapter 2, what favor does Mole ask of Ratty?
   a. to teach him how to write poetry
   b. to take him to meet Toad
   c. to take him to meet Badger
   d. to buy him a canary-colored cart

7. What season is the opening of Chapter 2?
   a. winter
   b. spring
   c. summer
   d. fall

8. What does Toad request of Mole and Ratty?
   a. to travel on the open road with him
   b. to help him repair the paddock at Toad Hall
   c. to ride in a motor-car with him
   d. to punt on the river

9. What literary device is used in "he proceeded to play upon the inexperienced Mole as on a harp"?
   a. allusion
   b. alliteration
   c. simile
   d. foreshadowing

10. What caused Toad's great epiphany?
    a. the canary-colored cart
    b. the rapturous simplicity of the primitive life
    c. the motor-car
    d. traveling by train

SHORT ANSWER

1. In a complete sentence, describe Toad's character. (2 pts.)

   <u>Answers will vary. Toad's character can be described as boastful, proud, and always looking for</u>

   <u>the latest and greatest. Toad is also very social and willing to share what he has with his friends.</u>

2. In complete sentences, explain how Toad's view of the open road changes. (3 pts.)

   <u>Answers will vary. Toad's view of the open road changes from the excitement for traveling to</u>

   <u>new places and seeing everything a new place has to offer, to simply wanting to speed down the</u>

   <u>open road as fast as he can, blowing past all the places he had previously wanted to experience.</u>

QUIZ: Chapters 3-4 — KEY

Name:_____ Date: _____ Score: _____

VOCABULARY: Choose the correct definition for the underlined word. (1 pt. each)

1. "the <u>languorous</u> siesta of hot midday"
   a. noisy
   b. disturbing
   c. long; dull
   d. weary; weak

2. "the <u>verdant</u> banks of dream-rivers"
   a. rusty
   b. copper
   c. green
   d. muddy

3. "'Really Rat,' said the Mole quite <u>pettishly</u>."
   a. cruelly
   b. giddily
   c. mockingly
   d. in a bad-tempered way

4. "the astonished and … <u>incredulous</u> Mole"
   a. unbelieving
   b. irresponsible
   c. mischievous
   d. overjoyed

5. "Rat attacked a snow-bank … with <u>ardour</u>."
   a. weariness
   b. enthusiasm
   c. great frustration
   d. warm delight

6. "he had been busy laying a <u>repast</u>"
   a. lawn
   b. blanket
   c. meal
   d. campsite

7. "The Mole <u>assented</u> heartily"
   a. disagreed
   b. ate vigorously
   c. agreed
   d. complained

8. "the whole mass of the Wild Wood, dense, <u>menacing</u>, compact"
   a. simple in design
   b. threatening
   c. disjointed
   d. expansive

9. "more to <u>oblige</u> the Rat than for any other reason"
   a. to be kindly accommodating
   b. to confuse by teasing
   c. to comfort because of sorrow
   d. to signal a warning

10. "I had to <u>cuff</u> his head once or twice"
    a. to strike with an open hand
    b. to pet with gentle affection
    c. to translate
    d. to fill in missing information

MULTIPLE CHOICE (1 pt. each)

1. What quality does Badger show when listening to Rat and Mole tell their story of how they got stuck in the woods?
   a. nervousness
   b. weariness
   c. wisdom
   d. impatience

2. After his experience in the Wild Wood, where does Mole learn that he belongs?
   a. in safe, domesticated places
   b. in a riverboat (Ratty was right all along!)
   c. at Toad Hall
   d. in wild, unknown lands

3. What does Mole like most about winter?
   a. hot apple cider
   b. the sound of the winter wind
   c. all the land uncovered and bare
   d. the beautiful snowfall

4. How is Mole best described?
   a. rude
   b. wise
   c. brave
   d. childlike

5. Who said, "Any friend of *mine* walks where he likes in this country, or I'll know the reason why"?
   a. Ratty
   b. Mole
   c. Badger
   d. Toad

6. About whom was Rat speaking when he said, "The best of fellows! But you must not only take him *as* you find him, but *when* you find him"?
   a. Toad
   b. Rabbit
   c. Otter
   d. Badger

7. About whom were the friends speaking when they said, "Smashes, or machines? ... O, well, after all, it's the same thing— with _____"?
   a. Badger
   b. Toad
   c. Otter
   d. Ratty

8. "Such a rich chapter it [the summer] had been" is an example of
   a. alliteration
   b. metaphor
   c. onomatopoeia
   d. simile

9. "Purple loosestrife arrived early, shaking luxuriant tangled locks" is an example of
   a. simile
   b. metaphor
   c. onomatopoeia
   d. personification

10. "diffident and delaying dog-rose stepped delicately" is an example of
    a. alliteration
    b. metaphor
    c. onomatopoeia
    d. personification

SHORT ANSWER

1. List the three clues Ratty uses to determine they are at Badger's door? (3 pts.)

   The three clues Ratty uses to determine they are at Badger's door are the door-scraper, the

   door-mat, and an iron bell-pull with a brass plate engraved with the name of Mr. Badger.

   _____

   _____

   _____

2. In a complete sentence, explain the common bond between Mole and Badger. (2 pts.)

   Answers will vary. The common bond between Mole and Badger is their love of the quiet

   security that comes with living underground.

   _____

   _____

QUIZ: Chapters 5-6 — KEY

Name:_____ Date:_____ Score:_____

VOCABULARY: Choose the correct definition for the underlined word. (1 pt. each)

1. "Close against the white blind hung a bird-cage, clearly silhouetted, every wire, perch, and <u>appurtenance</u> distinct and recognizable"
   a. accessory
   b. shadow
   c. curtain
   d. bar

2. "by a flow of cheerful talk and <u>anecdote</u> endeavoured to beguile his spirits back and make the weary way seem shorter"
   a. lavish attention
   b. a short humorous or interesting story
   c. a tall tale
   d. deep disdain

3. "The Badger's <u>caustic</u>, not to say brutal, remarks may be imagined, and therefore passed over"
   a. kind and compassionate
   b. lighthearted and witty
   c. sarcastic
   d. overly parental

4. Toad was accused of "gross <u>impertinence</u> to the rural police."
   a. outlandish trickery
   b. insulting, irreverent conduct
   c. improper physical appearance
   d. the act of fleeing arrest

5. "Poor Mole stood alone in the road, his heart torn <u>asunder</u>"
   a. deeply regretful
   b. discouraged; hopeless
   c. torn in two
   d. sorrowful; mournful

6. "No bread!" groaned the Mole <u>dolorously</u>
   a. hungry; famished
   b. sorrowfully; mournfully
   c. shamefully
   d. enthusiastically

7. "astonished and dismayed at the violence of Mole's <u>paroxysm</u> of grief"
   a. shame
   b. worriedness
   c. stoic response
   d. sudden outburst

8. "His hearty accents <u>faltered</u> and fell away"
   a. wavered; weakened
   b. strengthened
   c. came to a sudden end
   d. accused

9. "He did it awfully well," said the <u>crestfallen</u> Rat.
   a. proud
   b. ashamed
   c. determined; unrelenting
   d. heartfelt

10. "whom we see <u>cowering</u> in the dock before us"
   a. showing pride
   b. wincing as in pain
   c. crying uncontrollably
   d. crouching or shrinking away in fear

MULTIPLE CHOICE (1 pt. each)

1. What does the court say was Toad's worst offense?
   a. running away from home
   b. cheeking the police
   c. failing to pay his bill at the restaurant
   d. stealing the motor-car

2. What difficult choice does Mole have to make in Chapter 5: Dulce Domum?
   a. to move back home or to continue staying on the river
   b. to trust Ratty or to find his own way home
   c. to go find his home or to go on with Ratty
   d. to go through the village or to go through the fields

3. What do Toad's friends do when they realize he refuses to change his ways?
   a. They give up and leave him to his own foolishness.
   b. They remove him from Toad Hall.
   c. They imprison him in his room.
   d. They take him to a doctor.

4. What literary device is used here: "even the delicate tips of his plumped-out plumage pencilled plainly on the illuminated screen"?
   a. metaphor
   b. alliteration
   c. rhyme
   d. onomatopoeia

5. Where is Toad when he sees the fated motor-car that causes him such trouble?
   a. riding on a barge
   b. Red Lion
   c. on the river
   d. riding on a train

6. Which of the following is NOT a way that Ratty proves his friendship to Mole in Chapter 5: Dulce Domum?
   a. He tells Mole a bedtime story to help him sleep.
   b. He helps Mole clean and straighten his home.
   c. He backtracks in the cold to help Mole find his underground home.
   d. He sends out a field-mouse to buy food and drink for Mole's guests.

7. What does Ratty say when he realizes he has caused Mole's distress?
   a. "What a child you are being!"
   b. "What a *pig* I have been!"
   c. "I am sorry, old chap. Do forgive me and let's get to the river now!"
   d. "What on earth is causing such a commotion?"

8. What literary technique is used in the following passage: "'[Toad will] be so conceited … that he may commit any folly.' … So spoke the Badger, not knowing what the future held in store"?
   a. foreshadowing
   b. onomatopoeia
   c. personification
   d. metaphor

9. Which of the following is Toad called in court?
   a. a confounded coward
   b. the vilest of villains
   c. an ignorant fool
   d. an incorrigible rogue

10. What does the title *Dulce Domum* mean in Latin?
    a. Sweet Dome
    b. A Heart for Home
    c. Home Is Where the Heart Is
    d. Sweet Home

SHORT ANSWER

1. In complete sentences, explain three ways that Ratty shows his friendship to Mole in Chapter 5: Dulce Domum. (3 pts.)

   Ratty demonstrates his friendship to Mole in the following three ways: though Ratty wants to get home and eat, he realizes Mole is in distress and is willing to give up his own comfort to help Mole find his old home; he helps Mole clean up his home and cheers him up by asking him to recall memories of how he acquired certain objects; Ratty also plans and pays for a feast for the field-mice when they show up at Mole's door.

2. In Chapter 6, Toad is held accountable for his actions in a courtroom. While Toad receives time for stealing the car and endangering the public, his worst crime was "cheeking" the police. In complete sentences, explain the message Grahame was sending to his son through Toad's experience and consequences? (2 pts.)

   Through the courtroom scene, Grahame was sending his son the message that while consequences may be due for a wrong action, it is far worse to talk back to authority when you have done wrong. You will be given the greatest consequences for not showing respect and remorse rather than for the original mistake.

QUIZ: Chapters 7-8 — KEY

Name:_____ Date: _____ Score: _____

VOCABULARY: Choose the correct definition for the underlined word. (1 pt. each)

1. "till sunshine should fall on them at last and send them off to their well-earned <u>repose</u>"
   a. joy
   b. wages; payment
   c. rest
   d. meal

2. "some <u>august</u> Presence was very, very near"
   a. summerlike
   b. deserving of reverence
   c. ancient
   d. terrifying

3. "Toad found himself <u>immured</u> in a dank … dungeon"
   a. frozen
   b. hidden
   c. desperately lost
   d. enclosed

4. "with its [the breeze's] soft touch came instant <u>oblivion</u>"
   a. happiness
   b. total forgetfulness
   c. intense heat
   d. peaceful warmth

5. "in such an <u>audacious</u> manner"
   a. shy; timid
   b. rude or uncouth
   c. recklessly bold
   d. eager

6. "The chaff and the humorous <u>sallies</u> to which he was subjected"
   a. witty remarks
   b. long outings
   c. older sisters
   d. insults

7. "a <u>capricious</u> little breeze, dancing up from the surface of the water"
   a. steadfast
   b. constantly changing; unpredictable
   c. blustery
   d. cool and refreshing

8. "the only <u>stipulation</u> the old lady made being that she should be gagged"
   a. mix-up
   b. deviation
   c. joking
   d. condition in an agreement

9. "Toad was very much the same <u>sanguine</u>, self-satisfied animal"
   a. lazy
   b. picky
   c. outgoing
   d. melancholy

10. "a <u>jaunt</u> on the river"
    a. long journey; quest
    b. fishing expedition
    c. a holy journey
    d. short pleasure journey; outing

MULTIPLE CHOICE (1 pt. each)

1. When Chapter 7 begins, it is past ten at night and Mole is lying on the river bank when Ratty appears. From where had the Water Rat just come?
   a. a full day of boating on the river
   b. writing poetry
   c. dinner at Otter's house
   d. Wild Wood

2. Why are Ratty and Mole concerned about Little Portly?
   a. Otter has searched everywhere and has seen no signs of him.
   b. Portly is not a very good swimmer.
   c. There are traps.
   d. all of the above

3. What do Ratty and Mole do when they see the piper?
   a. They worship him.
   b. They ask him as many questions as they can about life.
   c. They call their friends to come see.
   d. They run and hide.

4. How does Toad escape the policemen who are chasing the train?
   a. He hides underneath the engine while it's moving.
   b. He jumps off into the woods.
   c. He pushes the engine-driver off and takes over.
   d. He hides in the coal piles.

5. How does Toad escape the dungeon?
   a. Ratty and Mole pay the judge to sign his release.
   b. He tunnels his way out through the floor.
   c. He knocks out the jailer and climbs out through the vents.
   d. He disguises himself as a washerwoman and walks out.

6. How does the piper ensure that the animals will still be happy after losing sight of him?
   a. He gives Ratty his pipes to keep.
   b. He gives them an autographed photo of himself.
   c. He makes them forget ever having seen him.
   d. He comes home to stay with them on the river.

7. Why does the gaoler's daughter want to help Toad?
   a. She falls in love with Toad and wants to marry him.
   b. She hates the prison warden and wants to cause problems.
   c. She's fond of animals and wants to teach him pet tricks.
   d. She thinks Toad is a famous war hero.

8. Who is the piper, and what is his relationship to the animals in the story?
   a. A farmer; he wants to take them as pets.
   b. Mr. Tumnus; he's a spying fawn.
   c. Pan; he's their god.
   d. The Pied Piper of Hamlin; he plans to lead them into the river.

9. What does the gaoler's daughter say is Toad's chief fault?

    a. He can't swim.

    b. He dreams too much.

    c. He's never happy.

    d. He talks too much.

10. How does Toad react when he first realizes he is in a dungeon?

    a. He throws a temper tantrum and refuses to eat.

    b. He swears to own the prison one day.

    c. He violently attacks the prison guard.

    d. He makes friends with his fellow prisoners.

SHORT ANSWER

1. Explain why Pan wipes the memories of the animals he helps. (2 pts.)

   Pan wipes the memories of the animals he helps because he knows that once they have been in his presence, they will never feel happy again.

2. In Chapter 8, the gaoler's daughter takes pity on Toad and brings him a tray of tea and toast. Grahame writes, "The smell of that buttered toast simply talked to Toad, and with no uncertain voice; talked of warm kitchens, of breakfasts on bright frosty mornings, of cosy parlor firesides on winter evenings." Using complete sentences, explain the literary device(s) Grahame uses in this passage. (3 pts.)

   Grahame uses several literary devices in this passage. One device he uses is imagery. He describes warm kitchens, bright frosty mornings, cozy parlor firesides, and the smell of buttered toast, all comforting things with which the reader would be familiar. Another device he uses is personification, when he writes that the buttered toast "talked to Toad." He has given the toast the humanlike quality of speech.

QUIZ: Chapter 9 — KEY

Name:_____ Date: _____ Score: _____

VOCABULARY: Choose the correct definition for the underlined word. (1 pt. each)

1. "The beat and quiver of impatient <u>pinions</u>"
   a. wings or feathers
   b. fingers
   c. a type of English leather shoes
   d. fleeting thoughts

2. "suggested the Water Rat <u>wistfully</u>"
   a. hopeless
   b. with sadness
   c. at ease
   d. worrisome

3. "now ere the <u>irrevocable</u> moment passes"
   a. reversible
   b. holy
   c. unable to be taken back
   d. temporary

4. "an <u>epitome</u> of my highly-colored life"
   a. ideal example
   b. opposite of
   c. distraction
   d. previous

5. "a <u>blithe some</u> step forward"
   a. mournful
   b. blundering
   c. hasty
   d. happy and lighthearted

MULTIPLE CHOICE (1 pt. each)

1. The title of Chapter 9 is "Wayfarers All." Who are the wayfarers?
   a. The animals boating on the river.
   b. The animals preparing to hibernate.
   c. The animals the rabbits charge to pass the road.
   d. The animals preparing to migrate to the south.

2. Why is the Water Rat feeling restless?
   a. There is a feeling of change in the air.
   b. He has writer's block and is struggling to write a new poem.
   c. The lack of rain has kept the river too low to go boating.
   d. There are too many animals at the river bank at this time of year.

3. "Nature's Grand Hotel has its Season" is an example of
   a. simile
   b. personification
   c. metaphor
   d. onomatopoeia

4. Which of the following does NOT cause Ratty to be "possessed" for a time by the Sea Rat's tales?
   a. the lights reflected in the Sea Rat's eyes
   b. the colored light of the red wine in the Sea Rat's glass
   c. the sea-foam grey-green of the Sea Rat's eyes
   d. the music of the Sea Rat's sailing song

5. When speaking about the farm and river life, what does the Sea Rat mean when he says, "It is a goodly life that you lead, friend; no doubt the best in the world, if only you are strong enough to lead it!"
   a. that farming is honorable but difficult and requires great strength
   b. that living tied to one place all the time takes strength
   c. that the river's ebb and flow require strength to manage
   d. that dealing with all the migration of animals coming and going takes strength

6. How is Ratty different in Chapter 9 compared to Chapter 1?
   a. He longs to see the Wide World now.
   b. He hates the river.
   c. He has grown tired of poetry.
   d. He begins to crave fortune and fame.

7. How does Mole prove to be a true friend to Ratty at the end of Chapter 9?
   a. He encourages Ratty to go to sea even though he will miss him.
   b. He calls Badger to help him run off the Sea Rat.
   c. He prays to Pan for Ratty to have a safe journey.
   d. He treats Ratty similarly to how they treated Toad, dragging him inside the house until he comes to his senses.

8. What does Mole do to help Ratty?
   a. He has Badger guard the door so he cannot leave.
   b. Mole gives him paper and encourages Ratty to write poetry.
   c. He gives Ratty a compass for his travels.
   d. He has the field-mice go to town and get Ratty's favorite treats.

SHORT ANSWER

1. In what season does this chapter take place, and how does this reflect Ratty's season of life? (5 pts.)

   Chapter 9 takes place in late summer/early fall when nature's bounty is full and ripe. It is

   before the migrating animals have headed south. They realize that the season will be changing

   soon and now is the time to get ready to go while they still can make the trip easily. This

   season reflects Ratty's life because he is healthy and full of life now, but knows the next

   season of life is old age and he will not be able to travel as easily. He wonders if he should go

   explore the Wide World while he still can.

2. When the swallows describe the pull of nature to the wonderful place in the south that they will be heading to, Ratty asks, "Why do you ever come back, then, at all?" What reason do the swallows give for their return? (2 pts.)

   The reason the swallows give for wanting to return to the river bank is that there is a season for

   everything. Just as the south calls now, there will be a time when they will remember the river

   bank with all of its joys and wonders and will feel called just as strongly to return home.

QUIZ: Chapters 10-11 — KEY

Name:_____ Date: _____ Score: _____

VOCABULARY: Choose the correct definition for the underlined word. (1 pt. each)

1. "he was determined to be <u>prudent</u>"
   a. smart-witted; good at making fun of others
   b. avoiding detection at any cost
   c. sly; sneaky
   d. careful; wise

2. "I simply <u>dote</u> on it [doing laundry]."
   a. to doubt or disbelieve
   b. to despise or fear
   c. to write upon
   d. to be overly affectionate toward

3. "its chill was not sufficient to <u>quell</u> his proud spirit"
   a. to quiet or calm
   b. to decrease
   c. to exaggerate
   d. to fill with pleasure

4. "the barge-woman was <u>gesticulating</u> wildly"
   a. stomping in quick rhythm
   b. making crude jokes; mocking
   c. making gestures with arms and hands
   d. a series of loud shouts

5. "<u>ignominiously</u> flung into the water"
   a. in a degrading way; shamefully
   b. absentmindedly
   c. with great pleasure
   d. to handle gently as with something that is fragile

6. "He's a good boy, but very light and <u>volatile</u> in character"
   a. shy
   b. easily angered
   c. not clever
   d. overly verbal

7. "such escapes, such disguises, such <u>subterfuges</u>"
   a. deceptive strategies for the purpose of escaping or evading
   b. daring efforts
   c. rough terrain
   d. difficult circumstances

8. "said the good-natured Rat, already <u>appeased</u>"
   a. showing signs of agitation
   b. nodding off to sleep
   c. calmed; made to feel better
   d. ready to defend

9. "with every fresh <u>accoutrement</u> he produced"
   a. idea
   b. verbal insult
   c. accessory item of equipment or dress
   d. confession of faith

10. "shaken by sobs of <u>contrition</u>"
    a. repentance; sorrow over one's sins
    b. anger or rage
    c. embarrassment
    d. frustration

MULTIPLE CHOICE (1 pt. each)

1. At the opening of Chapter 10, where had Toad spent the night after escaping the train?
   a. in an abandoned motor-car
   b. in a hollow tree
   c. in a gipsy caravan
   d. on a barge

2. Why does Toad have to do the barge-woman's laundry?
   a. because he boasted that he loved to do laundry
   b. because he lost a bet
   c. in exchange for a ride on the barge
   d. because he wanted to help her

3. "They [the garments] smiled back at him out of the tub unconverted, happy in their original sin." This sentence contains an example of
   a. imagery
   b. alliteration
   c. personification
   d. metaphor

4. Toad sells the horse to the gipsy because he wants
   a. a ride to Toad Hall and a new cart
   b. money and a solid breakfast
   c. breakfast and a ride to Toad Hall
   d. money in his pockets and revenge on the barge-woman

5. Who does Toad meet at the end of Chapter 10 in the hole on the river?
   a. Otter
   b. Badger
   c. Mole
   d. Water Rat

6. What news does Rat have for Toad?
   a. Portly is missing.
   b. Toad Hall has been overrun with Wild Wooders.
   c. There was a fire at Toad Hall.
   d. The police are waiting for him at Toad Hall.

7. "And a large tear welled up in each of his eyes, overflowed and splashed on the table, plop! plop!" This is an example of
   a. epiphany
   b. onomatopoeia
   c. simile
   d. plot

8. Badger reveals that a secret passage leads from the river bank to where in Toad Hall?
   a. the butler's pantry
   b. the dining room
   c. the library
   d. the dungeon

9. What celebration does Otter learn will be taking place in Toad Hall?
   a. Chief Weasel's wedding
   b. Chief Weasel's daughter's wedding
   c. Chief Weasel's birthday
   d. Chief Stoat's birthday

SHORT ANSWER

1. When talking to the barge-woman, Toad says, "I simply dote on it. Never so happy as when I've got both arms in the wash-tub. But, then, it comes so easy to me! No trouble at all! A real pleasure, I assure you, ma'am!" How does this reveal the chief fault of Toad, according to the gaoler's daughter? (3 pts.)

   According to the gaoler's daughter, Toad's chief fault is that he talks too much. In this

   passage, Toad boasts about how much he loves to do laundry and how happy it makes him. As

   a result, the barge-woman tells Toad to do her laundry because she never has time for it. Toad

   has bragged about how much he enjoys the work. Toad's boasting and bragging causes him to

   have consequences he did not want.

2. Why does Badger regard Mole as clever and not foolish when Mole tells the stoats about an impending attack? (3 pts.)

   Badger regards Mole as clever because he realizes that Mole is making all the guards nervous

   about a grand attack being planned as well as causing division among the weasels, stoats, and

   ferrets. Mole's actions are helpful when they attack from inside Toad Hall.

FINAL EXAM — KEY

Name:_____ Date: _____ Score: _____

VOCABULARY: Choose the correct definition for the underlined word. (2 pts. each)

1. "This was an impromptu affair"
   a. mocking
   b. careful
   c. crazy
   d. unplanned

2. "Naturally a voluble animal"
   a. stuffed
   b. proud
   c. hopeless
   d. talkative

3. "the astonished and ... incredulous Mole"
   a. unbelieving
   b. irresponsible
   c. mischievous
   d. overjoyed

4. "more to oblige the Rat than for any other reason"
   a. to be kindly accommodating
   b. to confuse by teasing
   c. to comfort because of sorrow
   d. to signal a warning

5. "No bread!" groaned the Mole dolorously
   a. hungry; famished
   b. sorrowfully; mournfully
   c. shamefully
   d. enthusiastically

6. "The Badger's caustic, not to say brutal, remarks may be imagined, and therefore passed over"
   a. kind and compassionate
   b. lighthearted and witty
   c. painfully sarcastic
   d. overly parental

7. "some august Presence was very, very near"
   a. summerlike
   b. deserving of reverence
   c. ancient
   d. terrifying

8. "a capricious little breeze, dancing up from the surface of the water"
   a. steadfast
   b. constantly changing; unpredictable
   c. blustery
   d. cool and refreshing

9. "an epitome of my highly-colored life"
   a. ideal example
   b. opposite of
   c. distraction
   d. previous

10. "a <u>blithe some</u> step forward"
    a. mournful
    b. blundering
    c. hasty
    d. happy and lighthearted

11. "<u>ignominiously</u> flung into the water"
    a. in a degrading way; shamefully
    b. absentmindedly
    c. with great pleasure
    d. to handle gently as with something that is fragile

12. "its chill was not sufficient to <u>quell</u> his proud spirit"
    a. to quiet or calm
    b. to decrease
    c. to exaggerate
    d. to fill with pleasure

13. "the Badger only remarked <u>placidly</u>"
    a. coldly
    b. absentmindedly
    c. calmly
    d. sarcastically

14. A series of actions or related events that move the story forward:
    a. foreshadowing
    b. irony
    c. plot
    d. setting

15. A reference to any person, place, or thing (literary, historical, or actual):
    a. allusion
    b. personification
    c. epiphany
    d. metaphor

MULTIPLE CHOICE (2 pts. each)

1. How has Toad's character changed by the end of the story?
    a. He gave up his longing for adventure for good.
    b. He asked Badger to move into his home and help him stay out of trouble.
    c. He learned to stop boasting and be humble.
    d. He gave away his home and went to live on the river.
    e. He grew weary of his friends' interfering and turned against them.

2. According to Ratty, "There is *nothing*—absolutely nothing—half so much worth doing as simply ..." Complete the quote.
    a. lying under the stars.
    b. walking about with friends.
    c. sculling about on the river.
    d. messing about in boats.
    e. writing great poetry.

3. After whom in Kenneth Grahame's world is Toad's character patterned?

   a. Grahame himself
   b. Grahame's son
   c. Grahame's alcoholic father
   d. Grahame's boss at the bank
   e. Grahame's younger brother

4. At one point in the story, Ratty changes his opinion about something in a significant way. What is it?

   a. He goes from being disgusted with Toad's behavior to admiring Toad's brilliant escape.
   b. He goes from loving the river to fearing water for a brief moment.
   c. He goes from being disinterested in the Wide World to longing to go to sea and experience it.
   d. He goes from loving boats to preferring motor-cars.
   e. He goes from not trusting Badger to being Badger's good friend.

5. Which of the following is an example of personification in *The Wind in the Willows*?

   a. "plumped-out plumage pencilled plainly"
   b. "scene-pictures that succeeded each other"
   c. "while the river still chattered on to him, a babbling procession of the best stories in the world"
   d. "not knowing ... how much water ... was to run under bridges before Toad should sit at ease"
   e. "the pageant of the river bank"

6. Which of the following is a metaphor in *The Wind in the Willows*?

   a. "Such a rich chapter it [the summer] had been."
   b. "Their old haunts greeted them again ..."
   c. "the whole mass of the Wild Wood, dense, menacing, compact"
   d. "So spoke the Badger, not knowing what the future held in store ..."
   e. "the diffident and delaying dog-rose"

7. What was Toad's epiphany?

   a. his open road experience with the canary-colored cart
   b. his life-changing vision of the motor-car
   c. his grand moment taking back Toad Hall with his friends
   d. his courtroom experience
   e. his near-death experience when he falls into the river

8. At the end of Chapter 4: Mr. Badger, where has Mole learned that he belongs?

   a. adventuring in the Wide World
   b. on the river
   c. with his friends, wherever they may go
   d. in domesticated, civilized places of tilled field and hedgerow
   e. in the Wild Wood with Badger

9. Which of the following is NOT one of Toad's character flaws or faults?

   a. He is cruel to his friends.
   b. He talks too much.
   c. He is greedy and covetous.
   d. He is impulsive—acts without thinking first.
   e. He has no self-control.

10. Which of the following is an example of alliteration from *The Wind in the Willows*?
    a. "a hot sun seemed to be pulling everything ... up out of the earth towards him"
    b. "the diffident and delaying dog-rose"
    c. "it is impossible to say quite *all* you feel when your head is under water"
    d. "The ruddy brick floor smiled up at the smoky ceiling"
    e. "The pageant of the river bank had marched steadily along"

11. Which of the following is meant to describe Pan?
    a. "let each one of the crowd try and shout it very loud, in honor of an animal of whom you're justly proud"
    b. "Helper and healer, I cheer—Small waifs in the woodland wet"
    c. "like the very soul of Nature ... appearing to her children, a true Goddess"
    d. "Yellow feet a-quiver ... Busy in the river!"
    e. "draw us in by your fire to bide; Joy shall be yours in the morning"

12. Which of the following best describes Badger?
    a. cruel and violent; a bully of sorts
    b. silent, angry, and pouty most of the time
    c. serious, unchanging, stern but kind
    d. outgoing, but not a good listener
    e. greedy, always wanting a bigger home

13. Which of the following is NOT a character quality of Ratty?
    a. loves to be on the river
    b. poetic
    c. always a faithful friend
    d. observant
    e. loves to party

14. What clever thing does Mole do in Chapter 11?
    a. He disguises himself as a washerwoman and feeds false information to the stoats, ferrets, and weasels.
    b. He helps Toad get through the underground tunnel to safety.
    c. He sneaks into Toad Hall and spies on the weasels as they make party plans.
    d. He finds a back entrance into Toad Hall that isn't guarded.
    e. He sneaks up on the ferrets and single-handedly steals away with their weapons without getting caught.

15. Which of the following best describes the way Mole changes from the beginning of the story to the end?
    a. He grows to hate living underground.
    b. He quits being so selfish and boastful.
    c. He becomes a fun-loving party animal.
    d. He learns not to be so trusting of others.
    e. He "grows up" and becomes a brave leader.

SHORT ANSWER

1. Why does Mole prefer the Wild Wood in the winter over the summer? (5 pts.)

   Mole prefers the Wild Wood in the winter because it is bare and open. He can see into its dark

   spaces that had been mysterious and hidden by the summer foliage.

2. The gaoler's daughter says that Toad's chief fault is that he talks too much. What is another fault Toad exhibits in the novel? Give an example to support your answer. (5 pts.)

   Answers will vary. Toad moves from one new interest to another without mastering anything.

   He is always looking for the latest and greatest thing. Toad's behavior is an embarrassment to

   the people who call him friend, and he does not really try to change. He is prideful and thinks

   himself better than others because he is a "many-pocketed animal."

3. Proverbs 17:28 says, "Even a fool, when he holdeth his peace, is counted wise: and he that shutteth his lips is esteemed a man of understanding." At what event does Toad finally apply this wisdom? How do Badger and Ratty respond to this new Toad? (5 pts.)

   At the end of the novel, Toad throws a party to give thanks to his friends for getting Toad Hall

   back. Rather than being his usual boastful self, Toad holds his tongue, allowing praises to only

   go to his friends. Ratty and Badger are both shocked and pleased with the new Toad.

ESSAY

1. In *The Wind in the Willows*, Grahame uses the four main characters to present a variety of life lessons and experiences. Choose a lesson that stood out to you. Give a brief summary of the events and characters involved. Explain both the lesson that Grahame is trying to convey and why you think this is an important lesson for a person to learn. (You may write in first person, as this is your opinion. There is not a right or wrong answer, only a supported or unsupported answer.) (15 pts.)

Answers will vary. Kenneth Grahame has filled *The Wind in the Willows* with advice and life lessons. One of the lessons that stands out to me occurs at the beginning of the book when Mole and Ratty are on the river and Mole has not yet learned to row or even to swim. Mole, being wise in his own eyes, takes the oars from Ratty and causes the boat to flip. Unable to swim, Mole must be rescued by Ratty, along with the picnic basket. Filled with shame for his actions, Mole apologizes to Ratty. Recognizing his inexperience, Ratty forgives Mole and offers to teach him how to row and swim. I believe the message that Grahame is giving the reader is that we need to learn from those who are wiser and more experienced, so that we do not suffer consequences. I also feel that Grahame is suggesting the mentor should be gracious and forgiving and help the inexperienced person learn from his mistakes. I believe this is an important message because we all have things to learn, and while learning by trial and error is an option, it is better to have a patient mentor to guide you through the process. Likewise, when we gain experience, we should be willing to help others the way we were helped. This is just one way that Grahame uses Mole and Ratty's relationship to teach many valuable lessons.